LIVING MISSIONALLY
BEYOND SUNDAY

...and all peoples will be blessed through you...
Genesis 12:3

KERRY D. M^C ROBERTS
FOREWORD BY CHARLIE SELF PH.D

Ark House Press
arkhousepress.com

© 2023 Kerry D. McRoberts

All rights reserved. Apart from any fair dealing for the purpose of study, research, criticism, or review, as permitted under the Copyright Act, no part may be reproduced by any process without written permission.

Scriptures taken from the Holy Bible, New International Version®, NIV®. Copyright © 1973, 1978, 1984, 2011 by Biblica, Inc.™ Used by permission of Zondervan. All rights reserved worldwide. www.zondervan.com The "NIV" and "New International Version" are trademarks registered in the United States Patent and Trademark Office by Biblica, Inc.™

Some names and identifying details have been changed to protect the privacy of individuals.

Cataloguing in Publication Data:
Title: Living Missionally Beyond Sunday
ISBN: 978-0-6456366-5-9 (pbk)
Subjects: Church; Missions; Christian Living;

Design by initiateagency.com

CONTENTS

Endorsements v
Foreword ix
Acknowledgements xi
Intro—Please Read! xiii

Chapter 1.   Prologue: There's Got To Be More! 1

Part 2.   Disciples Making Disciples

Chapter 2.   Challenging "Nest-Bound" Believers 13
Chapter 3.   God's "Handiwork" 24
Chapter 4.   Mission, Mission, Mission—Coupling Mission And Liminality 31
Chapter 5.   Incarnational Mission 43
Chapter 6.   Living Missionally Beyond Sunday! 56

Part 2.   Living Missionally Beyond Sunday!

Chapter 7.   The Missio Dei & A Missional Theology 71
Chapter 8.   The Underground Network 86

Chapter 9. Father's House 96
Chapter 10. Jacob's Well 105
Chapter 11. Kaleo Missional Communities 115
Chapter 12. Doxa Church 123
Chapter 13. Made To Flourish 128
Chapter 14. Victory Church 133
Chapter 15. Greenhouse Church 140
Chapter 16. "Third Places" 153
Chapter 17. Common & Unique Strands Of Missional DNA 167

Appendix 1—Disciples Making Disciples—Stage 5:
"Teaching Them To Obey…" 177
Bibliography 193

ENDORSEMENTS

"In the crowded big top of missional books, *Living Missionally Beyond Sunday* is up there on the highest wire, with Kerry McRoberts tossing from his tightrope wheelbarrow fresh insights on every page, scorning the safety net, and scoring big oohs and aahs from the reader from all the aha moments, ha ha ha!'s, take-aways, and move-forwards."

Leonard Sweet, author of 70 books, distinguished professor (George Fox University, Drew University, Kairos University, Northwind Seminary), and founder of SpiritVenture Ministries and The Salish Sea Press.

"I am convinced that a revived church is only possible through a rediscovery of our missionary identity. Kerry McRoberts has given us a book that not only re-centers mission for us but does so by engaging in a wonderfully thought-provoking blend of scripture (past) contemporary models (present) and forward thinking (future)."

Brian Sanders, Author and Founder and former Executive Director of the Underground Network; an international fellowship of microchurch incubators creating city-based ecosystems of faith, creativity, and empowered socio-missional enterprise.

"Kerry McRoberts believes that wherever a disciple is, they are always on mission. And to prove it he not only unpacks scripture and contemporary missional literature, but he tells the compelling stories of cops, bankers, tattooists, and a pastor with a barstool for a pulpit. He also interrogates the missional posture of faith communities like the Underground Network, Jacob's Well, Doxa, and a bunch of third place missions. A practical and informative primer on the mission of God's people.

Michael Frost, Morling College, Sydney. Author, *Shaping of Things to Come*, *Road to Missional*, and *Surprise the World*.

For,

Vic #867

FOREWORD

Dr. Charlie Self
Chief Intellectual Officer, Pathmakers Foundation
www.pathmakersfnd.org

Kerry McRoberts' work is an important godly provocation for the local church and all Christians who care about seeing their communities flourish spiritually and socially. In fact, one of the "O my!" insights in the book is that real spiritual awakening is not confined to religious gatherings…our joy in God's presence must translate to transformation in the community.

In every chapter "Mac" helps us end the unbiblical sacred/secular dichotomy as we realize that all we do is for God's glory and the good of others (Romans 12:1-2; Colossians 3:17ff). The author has done an amazing job of gathering and sharing insights from so many diverse leaders and organizations. From think tanks to local churches, non-profits and business leaders, there is a wealth of wisdom here. Most importantly, Mac is helping encourage a revolution in how we see our daily work as women and men on mission with the Lord.

This is not a refined academic treatise or a simplistic pop culture work. It is an enthusiastic exploration and unearthing of the biblical and empirical clarity we need to go forward in this VUCA (volatile, uncertain, chaotic, and ambiguous) world we are in. When all of God's people are on mission in all of life – especially their daily work – we can expect significant kingdom progress. All of the chapters have the unrefined freshness of Mac's humble inquiry and his ability to distill so much information in one place.

As a pastor and professor and leader in the faith and workspace for 30 years, I am grateful to commend this resource to all thoughtful leaders. Let the stories and wise learnings of godly women and men inspire your leadership and work. In the providence of God, this work, along with the efforts of many others, may be one catalyst in the coming awakening, where from the grassroots God's people become more attentive to God, better equipped for mission and work, and sources of love and wisdom in a world that is so broken and confused.

Buy and read this book…then buy several for your colleagues and friends. May the Lord bless our efforts in empowering all of God's people for Monday!

ACKNOWLEDGEMENTS

King David distinguished the sons of Issachar because they understood the times of uncertainty in which they lived, and they knew what Israel should do (1 Chron. 12:32). Whatever the merits of this book, some select people, who are among those, today, "who understand the times," and know what the church should do, have graciously contributed their insights to "*Living Missionally Beyond Sunday*": Dave Bennett, Wall Street banker and "Market-Place Pastor," Matt Haynes, owner of "Filament Tattoo Company," Jeff Hathcock, "the Barstool Pastor," and "Vic"—Vicki McRoberts, a police officer from Oregon, Tomy Wilkerson, Director, "The Underground," Pastor Steve Trujillo, "Father's House," Pastor Tim Keel, "Jacob's Well," Pastor Paul Hoffman, "Kaleo Missional Communities," Adam Hillyer, San Francisco Bay Area Director, "Saturate the World," Charlie Self, Professor, and Chief Intellectual Officer, Pathfinders Foundation, Jamé Bolds, Pastor, "Victory Church," Pastor Matt Ulrich, "Greenhouse Church," Bill Payne, Manager, "Ebenezers Coffee House," and Daniel Frederick, Executive Director, "The Coffee Oasis."

INTRO—*PLEASE READ!*

MISSIONAL LIVING IS A LIMINAL JOURNEY DOWN "A YELLOW-BRICK ROAD"

"You've always had the power, my dear, you just had to learn it for yourself." —Glinda, Oz's "Good Witch"

In his book, *The Forgotten Ways,* Alan Hirsch recalls to my memory certain details of a classic story that I have seen many times in black and white and in color over the course of my life, "The Wizard of Oz."[1]

The central character in the story is Dorothy, a young girl with long braided pigtails, who is swept away from her home in Kansas by a tornado to the magical land of Oz. Dorothy's all-consuming mission is to return home. Glinda, the "Good Witch" of the North, tells Dorothy to follow the yellow brick road to the Emerald City and there, she will meet the Wizard who will help her return home.

---

[1] Allan Hirsch, *The Forgotten Ways.* 21.

On her journey, Dorothy meets three peculiar characters who join her: The Scarecrow, who hopes the Wizard will give him a brain; a Tin Woodsman, who desires a heart from the Wizard; and a cowardly Lion, who wants the Wizard to give him courage.

But Dorothy, and her new companions, are severely tested with many trials in their journey to the Emerald City. The "Wicked Witch of the West" wants Dorothy's magic red slippers, and to get them, she causes extreme problems for Dorothy and her three companions, the Scarecrow, the Tin Woodsman, and the Cowardly Lion must together endure the Witch's evil spells, and aerial attacks from her nasty flying monkeys!

Nevertheless, Dorothy, the Scarecrow, the Tin Woodsman, and the Cowardly Lion survive everything the Wicked Witch opposes them with, and they finally arrive in Oz and come before the Wizard to make their requests for a brain, a heart, courage and means to go home to Kansas. As fiery columns border the massively projected head and face of The Wizard, he appears very frightening and fearful, until Dorothy's dog, Toto, rips the curtain down and exposes the Wizard as a fraud!

In despair, Dorothy, the brainless Scarecrow, the heartless Tin Woodsman, and the cowardly Lion leave Emerald City behind. But the Wicked Witch shows up and begins to make their lives even more miserable, she won't give up on trying to get Dorothy's red slippers. But Dorothy and her faithful companions overcome the Witch and her diabolical monkeys and liberate Oz.

All the trials, all the despair, discouragement and disappointment were necessary for Dorothy, the Scarecrow, the Tin Woodsman, and the Lion to realize that they did not need the Wizard after-all. Dorothy merely needed to realize that she was already equipped to return home, she just needed to click together the red slippers she had been wearing throughout her treacherous journey; the Scarecrow needed to use cleverness, understanding and instincts to cope with his journey, it then became self-evident to the Scarecrow that he had a brain; the Tin Woodsman discovered compassion that he was formerly unaware of; he really did have a heart, and the Lion was never without courage for together, they overcame evil and liberated Oz.

The "Wizard of Oz" vividly illustrates the biblical reality that every believer—e.g., carpenters, welders, loggers, police officers, physicians, custodians, lawyers, educators, truckers, farmers, ranchers, military personnel, bakers, etc., have "always had the power" to join God on His mission and transform their neighborhood, workplace, community, nation or world through the good works God prepared in advance for them to do but "[they] just had to learn it for [themselves]"—cf. Ephesians 2:10.

PART 1—DISCIPLES MAKING DISCIPLES

What is the mission of God in the world and what is my part in it? Chapter 1—Prologue: "There's Got To Be More," consists of four interviews with believers who are living missionally beyond Sunday! Driven by God's delivering love, these disciples obey Christ and "go" on their daily mission and work as a banker in the Wall Street industry, the owner of a tattoo company, a pastor with a barstool for a pulpit, and a police officer—*The life of each of these four people is a testimony to the daily reality that wherever a disciple is, they are always on mission.*

Part 1—"Disciples Making Disciples," develops five stages involved in disciplemaking: Chapter 2, Stage 1: "A Missionally-Driven Mindset," involves disciples moving from unawareness to soaring in their awareness of the biblical understanding of living missionally wherever they are. Chapter 3, Stage 2: "God's Handiwork" emphasizes the coupling of the disciple's work and/or daily activities with the works God prepared in advance for them to do (cf. Eph. 2:10). Chapter 4, Stage 3: "Mission, Mission, Mission—Coupling Mission and Modeling" highlights how Jesus makes disciples, "… he organizes it around mission"[2] (Alan Hirsch). Chapter 6, Stage 4: "Missional Incarnation" moves from Abraham's covenant with God, to Jesus' restoration of the Abrahamic Covenant to Luther's reinstatement of the consecration of all Christian disciples in the "Priesthood of All Believers" (1 Pet. 2:5; 9; Rev. 1:6).

As disciples go to "work in field and garden, in town and in house, in battling and in ruling," God is working through them to accomplish the Great Commission throughout every nook and cranny on earth (Cf. Matthew 28:18-20).

PART 2—LIVING MISSIONALLY BEYOND SUNDAY! MISSIONAL CONGREGATIONS & THE MISSIO DEI

"As the Father has sent me, I am sending you"

Missional Congregations, Organizations and "Third Places" are *sent*. In Part 2, pastors of missional congregations, directors of missional organizations and leaders/managers of third places are interviewed with the intent of bringing the reader into direct engagement with the culturally fluid (organic) nature of missional practice—The reader is asked to critically observe how these select missional congregations, organizations, and third places "live missionally beyond Sunday." And see, as well, how they engage and transform the cultural rhythms of their host communities by uniquely modeling a missional theology in imaginative, creative, and nuanced ways through incarnational mission.

---

[2] Allan Hirsch. *Forgotten Ways*. 120.

Part 2, Missional Congregations & The Missio Dei begins with a missional reading of Acts 8:1-25 and the formulation of a Missional Theology around its nucleus, The *Missio Dei*.

Chapter 8, "The Underground Network" is an authentically missional organization. My interview with Tomy Wilkerson, the Tampa Underground Director, contains multi layers of insight. The Underground's empowering structure for the purpose of effective disciplemaking is not only foundational for 75+ microchurches in Tampa, but for missional congregations in general.

Chapter 9, Father's House, draws the reader into the needed courage, persevering faith, and missional penetration into the chaos of Portland, Oregon by Pastor Trujillo and his missional congregation. Pastor Tim Keel, Jacob's Well, Chapter 10, provides a unique view of the transforming power of an "abiding church." Pastor Paul Hoffman, Chapter 11, provides a lucid portrait of missional praxis, both *proactive* and *reactive*. "Saturate the Sound" Director, Adam Hillyer, Chapter 12, highlights the amazing missional network and vision of SOMA Churches, locally and nationally. Charlie Self, Chapter 13, opened my eyes to new perspectives regarding the preparation of missional entrepreneurs, and the application of these perspectives by Pastor Jame Bolds, Chapter 14, has added significant value to his community. Chapter 15, Greenhouse Church, Gainesville, Florida, introduces Matt Ulrich, Pastor of Microchurches. Greenhouse uniquely and intentionally sees itself as a "both/and" church—This distinction is integral (and unique) to an understanding of the operations of Greenhouse Church, especially the penultimate enterprise of disciplemaking.

"Third Places," Chapter 16, are places where we spend our time when we have time off.[3] Ebenezars is located five blocks from the United States

---

[3] Alan Hirsch. *The Forgotten Ways*. 145.

Capitol Building in Washington D.C. Members of the U.S. Congress and homeless people (within a block of Ebenezars are poor neighborhoods) come together for their feet to be metaphorically washed by welcoming, compassionate missionally-driven believers. The Coffee Oasis, located in the "other Washington," is home to "the others," especially youth (18-25) with no one to care for them and the Berean House was a very small space, in a very small town where, in the early 80's God did amazingly big things despite a pastor who didn't "have a clue."

Chapter 17, "Common & Unique Missional DNA Strands," is a summation and illustration of the nuanced applications of a missional theology in Chapters 8 – 16. Appendix 1: Disciples Making Disciples—Stage 5: "Teaching Them To Obey"—The four stages of disciplemaking would be incomplete without Stage 5, ongoing study and fellowship of cohorts gathered to read and discuss missional theology and praxis in the works of gifted, seasoned writers, such as, Allan Hirsch, Michael Frost, Leonard Sweet, Brian Sanders and others.

CHAPTER 1

PROLOGUE: THERE'S GOT TO BE MORE!

> *"If the heart of discipleship is to become like Jesus, then it seems to me that a missional reading of the text requires that we see that Jesus's strategy is to get a whole lot of little versions of him infiltrating every nook and cranny of society by reproducing himself in and through his people in every place throughout the world"*—Alan Hirsch.[4]

What does a banker in New York City's Wall Street industry, the owner of Filament Tattoo Company in Indiana, a pastor with a bar stool for a pulpit in North Carolina, and a police officer in Oregon have in common? In a moment of spiritual crisis, they all shared in-common a notion something like, "there's got to be more!" What does that mean? They love Jesus and *people who don't*—that is, they "caught" a

---

[4] Allan Hirsch. *The Forgotten Ways.* 113. The following interviews, in this chapter, were by phone except for the last interview.

notion that they are to *go* and join Jesus on His mission and connect with people who are often very different from themselves.

"THE MARKET-PLACE PASTOR"

David Bennett is a banker in the Wall Street Industry in New York City. For the first sixteen years of his career, Dave was thoroughly conformed to the ego-driven, idolatrous, narcissistic culture of Wall Street. Nevertheless, Dave knew well how to use his vocation to generate revenue and make stockholders in major corporations wealthy. By Wall Street standards, Dave was successful.

Dave is the father of three children. When his children were young, he followed a family tradition in Greenwich, Connecticut and took them to church. The church Dave, and his family, began to attend experienced a crisis at the hands of an unscrupulous pastor. The consequences of the pastor's indiscretions were the leaving of the church by numerous families, to include Dave and his family.

Dave did not know where to go until a woman suggested that he try a church in Stanwich, Connecticut. Dave described his experience as being "hammered by the Holy Spirit" each time he and his family went to the church in Stanwich. For six weeks straight, the Spirit of God "hammered" Dave as he entered his new church—Dave experienced the Holy Spirit's baptism; but he did not understand what was happening to him and so, he asked the pastor, Chuck Davis, about it.

Pastor Davis explained to him that he was experiencing the presence of the Holy Spirit. The personhood and coequality of the Spirit with the Father and the Son was news to Dave then, but now, ten plus years later, Dave lives and works daily in the power of God.

Under Pastor Davis' care and leadership, Dave realized there's more to church than he ever imagined. Dave realized that God was willing to work through him to change the environment, and even the culture, of Wall Street. Daily, Dave intercedes in prayer for Wall Street leadership, employees, and clients. Dave often begins his day by asking God, "Who do you want to bless today, Lord?" And from among those he prays for, God gives him opportunity to pray one on one with them; he has seen many healed and he has led many to Christ, on the trading floor!

Like Joseph in ancient Egypt and Daniel in Babylon, God has given Dave favor with many executives in the Wall Street industry. God's favor gives Dave the liberty to not only openly pray with co-workers, and lead many of them to Christ, but also to pray for his co-workers and experience miraculous healings and deliverances from demonic bondage in their lives—Dave has become known as the "market-place pastor!"

While not at work, Dave ministers to the homeless and witnesses to gang members and leaders at high security prisons to include Rikers Island. One special story involves a homeless woman named Amy. For a couple of months, every morning, after getting off the subway and walking to work, Dave would stop and engage Amy in conversation—Amy was virtually invisible to the multiple thousands of people in Manhattan who would walk past her every day, except for Dave. Amy was only 30 years old, but she appeared much older, which is typical of most homeless people. Amy desperately wanted a home to live in. Before ending his conversations with Amy, Dave always prayed with her for a home.

One morning, as Dave was closing in prayer with Amy, a car drove up to the curb in front of them and a man got out of the car and walked up to Dave and Amy. The man worked for an organization that constructed housing for the homeless and provided mental health care and rehabilitation counseling to restore the homeless to society and work. Amy's prayers were answered, and she is now experiencing a restoration of her dignity and her place in society!

GOING TO THE COMMUNITY

For Matt Haynes, owner of Filament Tattoo Company, his reflections on, "There's got to be more …" began with his pastoring Calvary Baptist Church and his struggle to renew passion for the lost among his church members. Matt's congregation was unresponsive to his exhortations to reach the lost, they were content with being mostly rural families who liked each other and the patterns they had developed being a "church" more than they wanted to reach the lost.

Matt's frustration with his congregation led him to inform his administrative assistant that if anyone wanted to talk with him, "please have them call me on my cell phone, I'm moving my office to the coffee shop to be with people." Matt almost immediately discovered how genuine the Wabash community really was, they were caring and committed to the betterment of their town.

Matt also connected with a Wesleyan Pastor. New Journey Community Church was lively, impassioned and committed to reaching the unsaved in Wabash. (NJCC was a relative new church plant). Calvary Baptist Church had land, a building and money. The two pastors began sharing a vision for the uniting of their congregations.

Matt discussed his plans of a merger of New Journey Community Church and Calvary Baptist Church with his board and the Wesleyan Superintendent. Finally, the congregations of Calvary and New Journey joined with the two pastors to vote on the proposed merger. The merger failed by one vote.

Matt promptly stood before everyone and announced that he would "not pastor a church that refuses God's will." He then resigned as the pastor of Calvary Baptist Church. Matt humbly mentioned that several people came to his wife and him as they were leaving and informed them that they also were leaving and joining New Journey.

Two years before his resignation, Matt had spent time getting to know the owners of Studio B Tattooing. He worked the counter at Studio B for free, his benefit involved meeting and connecting with people, many of whom were outcasts and/or marginalized, that is, people disconnected from community life, socio-political involvement, and public networks and resources.

By means of God's provision, Matt was able to start Filament Tattoo Company as a new business in Wabash. Since then, the number of people Matt has connected with—in spiritually authentic ways—is "incredible!" For Matt Haynes, there is much more beyond Sunday!

THE "BARSTOOL PASTOR"

Jeff Hathcock, the Barstool Pastor, began thinking, "there's got to be more …" following an unfortunate clash with an influential person connected to ARP (Associate Reformed Presbyterian Church). Jeff was the Development Coordinator of Outreach North America. He was fresh out of the business world and new to church hierarchy, particularly, certain family names held in high esteem. Jeff was commissioned to develop an outreach program. [5] Following the completion of the writing of the program and the development of a DVD, Jeff was scheduled to present the new program to church leadership.

Present at the meeting was an individual whose family name required those present to revere him. This man did not like Jeff's approach to the project; and neither did he approve of Jeff's delivery. While quoting from

---

[5] Jeff's academic preparation for the ministry was with Reformed Theological Seminary, Charlotte, NC.

the Old Testament, he proceeded to verbally offer Jeff up as a type of "burnt offering" and dispose of him while those, who had commissioned Jeff to his work, sat in silence. Jeff left the church deeply wounded; he did not step foot in a church for two years.

During his absence from church, Jeff was contacted by a friend, Keith. Keith's fiancé, Michelle, worked at Our Place Bar in Charlotte, North Carolina. Michelle had recently died of stomach cancer. Keith told Jeff that he did not know any pastor and he did not have a church so, he asked Jeff to do Michelle's memorial service.

The memorial service took place in the back of Our Place Bar. Ninety-three people came to the service. The food was placed on a pool table covered with a tablecloth. All ninety-three people were without Christ, and therefore, without hope, but they sincerely loved Michelle and Keith.

Following the service, Jeff was seated in a corner of the bar and served a large plate of food. Person after person came to Jeff's table and told him how much they appreciated him for coming to them and sharing comforting words. Jeff was touched deeply by the authenticity of so many people—Jeff said to himself, "If Jesus is anywhere, He is surely in this place." Jeff had discovered that there is more, a lot more, beyond Sunday.

"Missional," according to Jeff, "is organic; it's not about 'build it and they will come,' it's about going to them, it's about taking the water to the desert—people walking into a bar know that they're sinners, I don't really know if people walking into a church know they are sinners."[6] Jeff added, I receive calls from people to come and pick them up and bring them to the bar. We will have a beer together while they explain to me how they used to go to church, but they were not welcome, there was no room for a drunk.

---

[6] Interview, Jeff Hathcock, January 14, 2019.

Jeff's website further says, "God doesn't quit on us. I won't either. This is a knee to knee ministry. My calling is to a one-on-one missional field to teach and reach the lost where they live." The Barstool Pastor offers individuals a safe one on one or small group setting to introduce, "the Jesus I know, the way He taught me…."[7] Once Jeff's church, in its tavern setting, grows to 50, he starts another "tavern church" with a pastor he has mentored.

How does Jeff see ministry from the vantage point of his barstool? Jeff's response centers on a question written on his website: "Sounds like a contradiction, doesn't it? Barstool and Pastor in the same sentence. How did the whole thing start? Well, I have a ton of experience in bars shooting pool and 'shooting the breeze.' The first ten years in the bar was for me. The next ten were for God. Think about it, you can walk into any bar in the world and order a beer and you're just like everyone else. Buy someone a beer and you're in the family."

"This is where real ministry meets real life and cultivates a conversational trust in Jesus. I walk beside and show up for men and women who have no pastor, church, or community group. From the hospital to the graveside, birth to baptism and every day in between. I offer what Jesus gave me, a place where I can pray for and love on those God puts in front of me. What I do, what God made me to do… is to take 'Living Water' to the thirsty sinner lost in the wilderness"—The Gospel is "For the Thirsty in All of Us."[8]

---

[7] Jeff Hathcock, Barstool Pastor, "Our Story," https://www.facebook.com/pg/barstool.pastor/about/?ref=page_internal. Downloaded, 01/14/2019.

[8] Ibid. Downloaded, 01/14/2019.

A COP ON MISSION

On a Sunday morning, my [the author] church was full, our budget's bottom line was well in the black, worship was lively, people were participating in the ministries of the church, and we were growing, people were *coming*. But, as I began to preach to a congregation I loved very much, I was surprised by a notion that flashed in my mind, "There's got to more!"

I could not shake this notion; it challenged my view of the relationship between Christ and culture, sacred and secular, mission, and ministry—My whole understanding of ecclesiology and mission was being radically challenged; this notion was unrelenting. I did not immediately realize where this notion had come from, although for the past few years it was embodied in front of me, to my right, every Sunday morning, wearing a police uniform, armed with a holstered 9 mm, Sig Sauer, and wearing a badge, # 867—"Vic", a respected, skilled, police officer, was serving and protecting Corvallis, Oregon, while simultaneously "taking water to the thirsty sinner in the wilderness," as Jeff Hathcock describes a missional vocation.

Vic connected with many different people, mostly, people who are not like her. She compassionately provided soul-care for female police officers; but she was also respected by male police officers, especially the "cowboys" on the midnight shift. Vic invited people into her home who had long since given up on the church; and the church had long since given up on them—*they were "the others."*

Vic eventually became the Crime and Intelligence Analyst for the Corvallis Police and the Benton County Sherriff Departments. She was also a member of a joint task force including the FBI, Oregon's Department of Justice, and the Oregon State Police.

Vic, additionally, was a city council member. And although she was often a lone "voice in the wilderness" among nine council members, she addressed city concerns with conviction, boldness, and intelligence. A Christian inserted into the politics of a [radically] liberal university community was not well received, at first. However, her ability to create environments for God to work through her, gave her access to the hearts of people politically, socially, and spiritually very different, and, very contrary, to herself—People were *coming* to our church, *but Vic modeled for me the "more" that deeply moved my heart, she was going* to people living on the edge of life where humanity is at the greatest risk.

In the context of the political life of the city, Vic's husband was not referred to by his name but as, "Vic's husband," by the Mayor, City Manager, members of the City Council, City Attorney, Chief of Police, and the Chief of the Fire Department. No wonder Vic's husband placed a personalized license plate on her car celebrating her "noble character"—PROV. 31.[9]

CONCLUSION: "THERE *IS* MORE!"

What does a banker on Wall Street in New York, the owner of Filament Tattoo Company in Indiana, the Bar Stool Pastor in North Carolina, and a police officer in Oregon have in common? *They all live missionally beyond Sunday!*

To live missionally is to daily join Jesus Christ on His mission, and for Him to work through missional-driven disciples so that "all peoples on earth will be blessed through you" (Gen. 12:3b). *Every believer—"from every nation, tribe, people and language"* (Rev. 7:9), is called to join God on His mission and live missionally beyond Sunday! (Cf. Mt. 28:18-20).

---

[9] Proverbs 31 is a beautiful picture of a virtuous woman.

PART 1

DISCIPLES MAKING DISCIPLES

CHAPTER 2

CHALLENGING "NEST-BOUND" BELIEVERS

Living missionally is for God's people to daily join Jesus on His mission; and for His mission to *engage* and *transform* the world *through* them![10]

"Disciples making disciples" is the penultimate enterprise of missional congregations. An extended illustration will be referenced throughout Part 1, "Disciples Making Disciples." This "extended illustration" will serve to crystalize how missional congregations obey Jesus Christ, to whom, "All authority in heaven and on earth has been given…," by going and making "disciples of all nations, baptizing them in the name of the Father, and of the Son and of the Holy Spirit," and "teaching them to obey everything" Christ has commanded us to do in five stages of disciplemaking (cf. Mt. 28:18-20).

---

[10] My definition of living missionally is shaped by Christopher J.H. Wright. *The Mission of God, Unlocking the Bible's Grand Narrative.* Downers Grove, IL.: Inter-Varsity Press, 2006. 22.

Chapter 2, "Challenging 'Nest-Bound' Believers," introduces Stage 1: "Nest-bound" believers resist joining God on His Mission. Chapter 3, "God's Handiwork," presents Stage 2: *"Born to Fly"*—Coupling Mission and Vocation. Chapter 4, "Mission, Mission, Mission," focuses on Stage 3: *"Modeling Flight"*—repetitious mission, coupled with modeling, are catalytic in the making of disciples. Chapter 5, "Incarnational Mission," highlights Stage 4: "Soaring 'In the Zone"—"The Royal Priesthood" of *all* believers. And Appendix 1, Stage 5: "Teaching Them To Obey," involves ongoing *koinonia* (Christian fellowship) and theological formation among missional-driven disciples of Jesus Christ.

THE LORD USES PAIN, TURMOIL AND LOSS TO FORCE US TO SOAR[11]

> *"Like an eagle that stirs up its nest, that flutters over its young, spreading out its wings, catching them, bearing them on its pinions, the Lord alone guided him…"*—Deut. 32:11-12.

As the mother eagle treats her young, so does God treat us. An eagle builds her nest high atop a tree or a cliff to protect her young from predators. The eagle will line the nest with the skins of animals she has killed, providing a covering over the sharp sticks. She will then pull feathers out of her own breast and line the nest with them to make a safe, warm, and protected place for the eggs.

---

[11] Don Ross. "Theology of Change – A Message from Network Leader, Don Ross." https://vimeo.com/412477594. Downloaded: 05/04/2020. Don Ross, Network Leader, Northwest Ministry Network of the Assemblies of God, used this illustration to introduce a discussion about COVID 19. But I am using this illustration, with Superintendent Don Ross' permission, to introduce disciplemaking in relation to liminal circumstances on mission.

The mother provides every need for her young. And she leaves the nest only when she needs to get more food for them—the eaglets want for nothing and they expect their mother's caring ways to continue, unchanged into the future.

But eagles were not born to live in a nest, they were born to fly, and the mother knows this. When the young eagles have grown feathers, the mother coaxes them to the top, to the edge of the nest to fly. The mother challenges her young to step out of the nest and fly, but they are afraid, and they resist.

For the eaglets, this is new, it is different, it is unfamiliar, and they are fearful. The first time they look over the edge of the nest, they see a world they cannot conceive, and they do not know what to do.

The mother is determined to make the eaglets fly, she then removes the feathers from the lining of the nest and the eaglet's world becomes colder. The mother again coaxes her young to the edge of the nest. And if the eaglets still resist their mother's promptings to fly, she removes the skin from over the sharp sticks, making the young eagle's habitat increasingly uncomfortable.

But, many times, young eagles will still refuse to leave the nest and soar in flight and so, the mother will begin dismantling the nest, stick by stick until there is hardly any nest and the eaglets have no choice but to begin to spread their wings.

A theological insight regarding the value of liminality is apparent: God will use pain, turmoil, and loss as reliable teachers—*When the pain becomes acute, we become open to change.*[12]

When the mother eagle finally succeeds in getting the eaglet to the top of the nest, she then launches into the air, showing her young what is pos-

---

[12] Don Ross. "Theology of Change – A Message from Network Leader, Don Ross."

sible when they step out of the nest and do what eagles were born to do. When the mother returns to the nest, she begins nudging her young to the edge of the nest, but they are scared, and they resist, however, the mother eagle is relentless; she knows their capability more than they do. And she tips them over the edge and into the air.

For the first time, the eaglets feel the air flowing through their wings, it's a new sensation but as they look at the ground far below, they become fearful of falling to their death, but the mother, in the last moment, swoops down and catches them on her back. And she returns them to what is left of the nest.

This painful, scary process is repeated until the eaglets learn to fly and then, a whole new world opens-up to them—the mother has used pain, fear, and modeling to transform fearful, nest bound eaglets into soaring young eagles.

STAGE 1: CHALLENGING "NEST-BOUND" BELIEVERS

"Nest-bound" believers resist joining God on His mission (*MissioDei*) — These believers just *"don't know that they don't know."*[13]

> *"But eagles were not born to live in a nest, they were born to fly, and the mother knows this. When the young eagles have grown feathers, the mother coaxes them to the top, to the edge of the nest to fly. The mother challenges her young to step out of the nest and fly, but they are afraid, and they resist."*

---

[13] Jeff Vanderstelt. *Building A Missional Community*, Part 1. https://www.youtube.com/watch?v=x8Inw0YchwM, Downloaded: 02/05/2019. Vanderstelt insightfully identifies this phase as: **"Unconscious/Incompetent."** Three following phases (featured in chapters 3-5) are identified by Vanderstelt as: **"Conscious/Incompetent," "Conscious/Competent"** and **"Unconscious/Competent."**

> *How are disciples challenged to "step out of the nest"? In other words, how does Christian leadership challenge the mindset of "nest-bound" believers who are unaware and therefore, unprepared for missional understanding and praxis?* [14]

Dorothy Sayers bluntly points to an unbiblical concept that has been (for over two centuries in North America, and over five centuries in Western Europe) buried in the psyches of a significant portion of the church: "In nothing has the Church so lost her hold on reality as in Her failure to understand and respect the secular vocation. She has allowed work and religion to become separate departments, and is astonished to find that, as a result, the secular work of the world is turned to purely selfish and destructive ends, and that the greater part of the world's intelligent workers have become irreligious, or at least, uninterested in religion… How can anyone remain interested in a religion which seems to have no concern with nine-tenths of his life?"[15] *How should Christian leaders "respect the secular vocation"? And how does Paul's view of reality relate to "the secular vocation?"*

REALITY IS COUPLED

"In the beginning God created the heavens and the earth" (Gen. 1:1). Creation is a series of binary relationships in Genesis 1—"the heavens and the earth" (1:1), "light and darkness" (1:4), "land and seas" (1:10), "evening

---

[14] See Clifford Hill, *The Wilberforce Connection*. Oxford, UK, Monarch, 2004. 359ff, for an historical connection to this problem.

[15] Dorothy Sayers. "The Secular Vocation is Sacred, Serve God in Your Profession, Not Outside It." April 1942. https://renovare.org/articles/the-secular-vocation-is-sacred. Downloaded: 10/15/2021. See also, Francis A. Schaeffer, Book Two: *Escape from Reason*. 207-236. The Complete Works of Francis A. Schaeffer, A Christian Worldview. Volume 1, A Christian View of Philosophy and Culture. Second Edition. Westchester, Illinois, Crossway Books, 1982.

and morning" (1:13), "day and night" (1:14), male and female (1:27).[16] All these relationships are intended by God to work together—*The nature of creation, and how God has designed the cosmos to work, relates to these couplets.*[17]

By the Word creating (Jn. 1:3)[18], God spoke these binary relationships into existence, and He pronounced that His creation is "good" (Genesis 1:3, 9, 12, 18,21, 24, 31). Specifically, God pronounced that the coupling of "the heavens and the earth," that is, the reality of the physical (empirical) world and metaphysical (spiritual) reality, the heavens, existing together as an undivided, organic whole is "good." This realization prompts us (in the West) to say, "I now see reality (creation) in terms of a post-secular worldview."[19] Allow me to further explain this conclusion and develop why it is important to a missional theology.

In Paul's day, acknowledges N.T. Wright, religion involved "… God related activities that, along with politics and community life, held a culture together and bound the members of that culture to its divinities and to one another. For Paul, 'religion' was woven in with all of life; for the modern Western world, it is separated from it."[20]

---

[16] The perceptive reader will acknowledge that same-sex marriage is a perversion of God's created order (cf. Romans 1:18-32). For further discussion, please see my book: *Insanity, How Can Sanity and Civility be Restored to a Culture in the Process of Being Turned Over to Itself?* pages 35-36; 39-45.

[17] My thinking here was inspired by: N.T. Wright. Same-Sex Marriage. https://www.youtube.com/watch?v=xKxvOMOmHeI. Downloaded: 04/19/2019.

[18] J.I. Packer. *Knowing God.* Downers Grove, IL.: Inter-Varsity Press, 1973. 56.

[19] The philosophical "uncoupling" of creation's complimentary relationship of "the heavens and the earth," into sacred and secular, creates opposing categories (sacred and secular) contrary to God's purpose in creation. Such a philosophical "uncoupling" is a perversion of God's good purposes for His creation, and therefore, a gross distortion of the nature of Biblical Revelation and consequently, reality.

[20] N.T. Wright. *Paul, A Biography.* 3.

For "the modern Western world, it is separated from it," that is, in the thinking of the modern Western world, "the heavens and the earth" (among the other binary relationships in creation) are uncoupled. This results in the division or separation of sacred and secular. Reality has not changed, but a philosophical shift birthed by French Enlightenment philosophers, e.g., Descartes, Voltaire, Rousseau, and British Empiricists, e.g., Locke, Hume, Berkeley, not to mention the German philosopher, Immanuel Kant, has produced a false view of reality, a view that uncouples "the heavens and the earth" into sacred and secular spheres.[21]

And consequently, we read Scripture in a way that justifies Dorothy Sayer's indictment of the Church—*We fail to read the Scriptures missionally and therein, we conclude that the work of the clergy is exalted to creation's "upstairs department," that is, the sacred, but the work of everyone else in the church is reduced to the "downstairs" of creation, i.e., the irreligious basement of a "secular vocation."*

Finally, three creation ordinances in Genesis are conceived by the binary relationships in creation: The preservation of marriage between one man and one woman, the necessity and propriety of work, and the keeping of the Sabbath (Genesis 2:1-3, 15, 18-24). God stitched these ordinances into the fabric of His creation.

Because work, specifically, is divinely "stitched into the fabric of His creation," it is sacred—All legitimate (legal/moral) work is sacred. Adam's work as a gardener and a landscaper was sacred; the eternal Word, through whom all things were made (Jn. 1:3) was a carpenter, by trade, and he did not hesitate to call as his disciples, fishermen, tax-collectors, physicians and by both implication and through his disciples, also soldiers.

---

[21] This view of "reality" is referred to as modernism. Modernism was birthed at the time of America's inception in late 18th century.

Christopher Wright contributes to our biblical understanding of the sacredness of work: "This delegated authority within the created order is moderated by the parallel commands in the complementary account, 'to work ... and to take care of' the Garden (Gen. 2:15). The care and keeping of creation is our human mission. The human race exists on the planet with a purpose that flows from the creative purpose of God himself. Out of this understanding of our humanity… flows our ecological responsibility, our economic activity involving work, productivity, exchange and trade, and the whole cultural mandate. To be human is to have a purposeful role in God's creation."[22]

RECOUPLING "THE HEAVENS AND THE EARTH"

> *"There are no unsacred places; there are only sacred places and desecrated places."*[23]

A missional practitioner does not see the world in terms of a "sacred/secular divide" but rather, "the heavens and the earth" are coupled.[24] A *post-secular* view of reality is critical to our understanding of the theological implications of the Incarnation, specifically regarding missional patterns in the ministry of Jesus Christ and his modeling of missional praxis for the church.

Pastoral leadership needs to begin "removing feathers from the lining of the nest" and creating a "colder" environment for the "nest-bound" believer. That is, pastoral leadership needs to move the believer to "the edge

---

[22] Christopher Wright. *The Mission of God.* 65.
[23] Wendell Berry. "There Are No Sacred and Unsacred Places https://kimmysophiabrown.com/mo-bliss/a-contemplation-of-nature-and-spirituality/wendell-berry-there-are-no-sacred-and-unsacred-places/. Downloaded 10/22/2021.
[24] Evil is not the opposite of good as though it exists as a separate entity, it is the spoiling of good (Augustine). Therefore, sacred, and desecrated are not opposites (as is the case with a sacred/secular divide) rather desecrated is, as defined, the perversion or spoiling of the sacred. Culture is therefore redeemable.

of the nest" [the pew] through, first, a missional reading of Scripture (I will provide examples of a missional reading of Scripture, and as well, recommended reading, in forthcoming chapters, especially, Chapter 7, "The *Missio Dei* and Missional Theology" and Appendix 1, "Disciples Making Disciples," Stage 5: "Teaching Them To Obey…").

Regarding the structure of a missional reading of Scripture, Christopher Wright explains the significance of the coupling of Jesus' messianic identity and His missional purpose by stressing that, "in the light of the story that leads *up to* Christ (messianic reading) and the story that leads *on from* Christ (missional reading) …, the story that flows from the mind and purpose of God in all the Scriptures, for all the nations…, is a missional hermeneutic of the whole Bible."[25]

Scripture—more specifically, a missional reading of Scripture—works as exposed sharp sticks, cf. Heb. 4:12.[26] A missional understanding of Scripture will equip the believer with lens necessary to "see" how God is a missional (i.e., "sending") God—*An initial change of mindset by means of a missional reading of God's word, prompts the disciple to look over the edge of the nest.*[27]

Once the unaware and/or resistant believer is "coaxed to the top, to the edge of the nest to fly," their spiritual imagination will be invoked, and they will become less fearful to the notion of the *Missio Dei*. They will then

---

[25] Ibid. 41.
[26] Re: footnote 24, I both will provide examples of "missional readings of Scripture," and academic opportunities/resources available to teach the reader (the student of missional praxis) how to read scripture missionally.
[27] "A *biblical basis of mission* seeks out those biblical texts that express or describe the missionary imperative, on the assumption that the Bible is authoritative. A *missional hermeneutic of the Bible,* however, explores the nature of biblical authority itself in relation to mission." Christopher Wright. Ibid., 51.

begin to be prepared for a journey where much, if not all, will be new to them and initially, they will not know what to do.

CONCLUSION—STAGE 1: CHALLENGING "NEST-BOUND" BELIEVERS

Mother eagles and educational theorists both recognize that there is a difference between "cognitive" (knowledge based) learning (or in the case of eaglets, instinct) and skills-based learning (for eaglets, watching mom fly and, for missional practitioners, watching seasoned practitioners model missional engagement, Stage 3) and "affective" (value-based) learning—... *eagles were not born to inhabit a nest, but to fly, and likewise, disciples are not called to merely occupy a stationary spot in a congregation but "to go and make disciples."* [28]

It is one thing to teach disciples what missional praxis is, but it is another to inspire them to be highly motivated, impassioned missional practitioners. The transforming of a disciple from a "nest-bound" bystander to a soaring, dynamic practitioner—a disciple who actively makes disciples, (Stage 4), begins with a missionally driven/biblically based transformation of the disciple's mindset (Stage 1).

Summarily, the objective of Stage 1 is to challenge the "nest-bound" believer to pivot his or her mindset from a centripetal view, that is, a "church-centric" perspective, to a centrifugal view—Mission is Christo-centric and therefore, it flows from the metaphysical ("the heavens") into the empirical (earthly/historical) rhythms of everyday life, and brings transformation to God's creation

---

[28] The three differences regarding educational theory are the work of: Jason Broge. "Affective Learning: How Congregants Move from Passion to Action." *Better Together, How Christians Can be a Welcome Influence in Their Neighborhoods.* Barna Group, 2020, 34.

through missional practitioners (A missional reading of Acts 8:1-25 in Chapter 7 will vividly illustrate this summary conclusion).

TRANSITION: MAKING DISCIPLES—STAGE 2

Jeff Vanderstelt describes the Second Stage of a disciple's missional awareness development, as **Conscious/Incompetent.**[29] Stage 2 inquires: *"Why does my work matter to God?"* And *"Why does God matter to my work?"*

---

[29] Jeff Vanderstelt, *Building A Missional Community,* Part 1.

CHAPTER 3

GOD'S "HANDIWORK"

STAGE 2: ***"BORN TO FLY"***: "I realize I really don't know"[30]

> *"… eagles were not born to inhabit a nest, but to fly…"*

Work is a sacred ordinance, and God intends for your vocation, your work, to be coupled with mission—"This is in accord with the profound New Testament concept that all the good works of the righteous are the work and gift of God."[31]

Therefore, every believer is to involve themselves "… in the eternal purposes of God in the world to redeem it to Himself, to sum up all things to Himself in Christ Jesus"[32]—For the creation ordinance of work to possess

---

[30] Jeff Vanderstelt. *Building A Missional Community,* Part 1. https://www.youtube.com/watch?v=x8Inw0YchwM, Downloaded: 02/05/2019. Vanderstelt describes this phase of a disciple's growing awareness of missional praxis as "Conscious/Incompetence," hence, "I realize I really don't know."

[31] *Theological Dictionary of the New Testament.* Vol. 5, 21.

[32] Allan Hirsch. "What is Missional Discipleship?" https://www.youtube.com/watch?v=WhEwxSQ5tqA. Downloaded: 02/28/2019.

ultimate purpose, passion and an abiding sense of mission, believers must *transform* their vocation into a *missional vocation*.

COUPLING MISSION AND VOCATION

May the favor of the Lord our God rest on us; establish the work of our hands for us—yes, establish the work of our hands" Psalm 90:17

God has called *all* believers—those who are "in Christ" by grace, through faith—to couple their daily work and lives with God's mission: "For we are God's *handiwork*, created in Christ Jesus to do good works, which God prepared in advance for us to do," Eph. 2:10.

The Greek term translated "handiwork" means "he has made us what we are."[33] God has blessed you with gifts, talents, skills, and passion to do the work you love—e.g., mechanic, welder, teacher, construction, custodian, farmer, logger, physician, grocery clerk, lawyer, nurse, bank teller, business owner, police officer, marine, soldier, airman, sailor, writer, musician, artist, etc. And God created you "in Christ" (you are a new creation[34]) to do good works, which God "prepared in advance," that is, before "the creation of the world."[35]

Tim Keller observes that, "Your vocation is a part of God's world in the world…." Your "life is not a series of random events. Your family background, education, and life experiences—even the most painful ones—all

---

[33] Grk. ποιέω. BAGD, 683.
[34] Grk. κτίζω. Ibid., 455.
[35] Grk. προετοιμάζω. Johannes P. Louw and Eugene A. Nida. *Greek-English Lexicon of the New Testament, Based on Semantic Domains*. Vol. 1, 683. BAGD, 705.

equip you to do some work that no one else can do."[36] Our daily work (and as we daily, just go about doing life), is to be complimented by its relationship with the works God has prepared for us to do before the creation of the world.

What are these "good works," "prepared in advance" by God for us to do? How do these "good works" relate to a missional vocation? And how do we access and dynamically apply these good works to living missionally and glorifying Christ in the office, on the work site, and in the marketplace?

"GOOD WORKS GOD PREPARED IN ADVANCE"?

After about a year of public ministry, Jesus returned to his hometown, Nazareth. On the Sabbath day, Jesus went to the synagogue. Typically, seven persons were asked to read portions of Scripture and because of his widespread reputation, Jesus was included among those invited to speak. In the presence of less than fifty people, he read from the prophet, Isaiah:

> *"The Spirit of the Lord is on me,*
> *because he has anointed me*
> *to proclaim good news to the poor.*
> *He has sent me to proclaim freedom for the prisoners*
> *and recovery of sight for the blind,*
> *to set the oppressed free,*
> *to proclaim the year of the Lord's favor."*

After rolling up the scroll, Jesus handed it to the attendant, and he sat down. The eyes of everyone in the Synagogue were eagerly fixated on Jesus

---

[36] Tim Keller, "Discerning Your Calling," https://www.whatsbestnext.com/2011/08/tim-keller-on-discerning-your-calling/, August 23, 2011, Matt Perman, Downloaded: 02/20/2019.

(Lk. 4:20).[37] And Jesus promptly announced, *"Today this scripture is fulfilled in your hearing"* (Lk. 4:21).

Instead of an apocalyptic pronouncement of the total doom of Israel's enemies, Jesus' mission is to go, and both preach the good news and do justice on behalf of the "oppressed," "the poor," "the prisoners," and "the blind;" these are examples of human misery,[38] these are the powerless, and the disenfranchised. The works the preincarnate Word, Jesus Christ, prepared for us to do before the creation of the world (Eph. 2:10) are disclosed in His Incarnation, specifically here, in Isaiah's prophetic announcement of the Messiah's mission (Isa. 61:1-2).

Additionally, in Matthew's Gospel (11:1-4), John the Baptist, in the tradition of the righteous prophets before him (Matt. 23:29-35), has been imprisoned and would soon be executed (cf. Matt. 14:1-12). John sends his disciples to Jesus to ask him, "Are you the one who is to come, or should we expect someone else?" (Matt. 11:3). Jesus' assurance of John that his death will not be in vain involves him pointing to the works Isaiah said would be done by the Messiah (Isa. 35:5-6): *⁴ "Go back and report to John what you hear and see: ⁵ The blind receive sight, the lame walk, those who have leprosy are cleansed, the deaf hear, the dead are raised, and the good news is proclaimed to the poor. ⁶ Blessed is anyone who does not stumble on account of me"* (Matt. 11:4-6)—The primary revelation of the Messiah is in His works.[39]

In John 14:12, Jesus says that those who believe in him, will do the works he has "been doing, and they will do even greater things than these, because I am going to the Father." The works Jesus has done, are the works

---

[37] A.T. Robertson. *Word Pictures in the New Testament, Luke, II.* 57.

[38] BAGD, Greek: αιχμάλωτος – beggars, blind men, and oppressed as examples of misery, Luke 4:18, 27.

[39] *Theological Dictionary of the New Testament.* Editors: Gerhard Kittel, Gerhard Friedrich. Grand Rapids, MI.: Wm. B. Eerdmans, 1971.Vol. VII, 248.

of God, and after Jesus ascends to the right-hand of the Father, these works will become, "… a testimony to the divine work in man."[40]

Moreover, because Jesus has gone to the Father, believers will do "even greater things" than Jesus.[41] The Greek term translated "greater" (μείζονα) does not mean surpassing in terms of quality but rather, in terms of quantity or scope. The Father and the Son, following Jesus' ascension, have sent the Spirit, and the Spirit both sends and leads the church in the implementing of the works of Jesus throughout the earth and in all generations (John 14:16-17; 15:26-27; 16:13-15).[42]

Conclusively, because Jesus has gone to the Father, the works done by believers in this life, are the "good works" prepared by God (Eph. 2:10).[43] The works God "prepared in advance" (before the creation of the cosmos) for believers to do (Eph. 2:10), explicitly include works of justice and mercy in behalf of the marginalized—setting free the "oppressed," "the poor," "the prisoners," and "the blind" (Lk. 4:16-17/Matt. 11:4-6); gifts to serve and care for the body of Christ (Rom. 12:3-8), the charismatic gifts (1 Cor. 12:1-11), and church leadership, "… the apostles, the prophets, the evangelists, the pastors, and teachers, to equip his people for works of service, so that the body of Christ may be built up…" (Eph. 4:7-9).[44]

Believers living missionally beyond Sunday—"missional practitioners"—see life through the lens of a post-secular reality, they therefore,

---

[40] *Theological Dictionary of the New Testament.* Grand Rapids, MI.: Wm. B. Eerdmans, 1968. Vol. VI, 482.
[41] Ibid.
[42] Ibid. Also, *Theological Dictionary of the New Testament,* Vol III., 1965,789, n.17.
[43] *Theological Dictionary of the New Testament.* Grand Rapids, MI.: Wm. B. Eerdmans, 1964. Vol. II, 705.
[44] Ibid. Also, *Theological Dictionary of the New Testament,* Vol. IX, 1974, 569.

see their vocation as a sacred calling, no less than their pastor's calling to his vocation.[45]

> ***"BORN TO FLY"***—*Believers were born-again to fly!*

In the likeness of the cast of the *Wizard of Oz,* the Scarecrow, the Tin Man and the Cowardly Lion, God's people, without exception, already possess within themselves the "good works" (Eph. 2:10) that enabled the primitive church in Acts to dramatically change the world for Christ.

"*I realize I really don't know*"—Such a notion acts as a flashpoint of awareness in a believer's conscience. Biblical clarity regarding two questions is essential to our understanding of how God intends for us to do the "good works" which He "prepared in advance for us to do" (Eph. 2:10): (1) *Why does my work matter to God?* And (2) *Why does God matter to my work?*

"INTEGRATORS," "COMPARTMENTALIZERS" AND "ONLOOKERS"

Barna researchers distinguish Christians and how they see their work in three categories: Integrators, Compartmentalizers and Onlookers.[46] The people described above (Prologue—Chapter 1)—David Bennett, Matt Haynes, Jeff Hathcock, and "Vic" McRoberts, are "Integrators," Christians who clearly see that their work serves God, shapes the culture of their workplace, and impacts the lives of fellow employees, clients, customers,

---

[45] Whereas the calling of a carpenter, construction worker, farmer, physician, attorney, police officer is no less sacred, and therefore, *equal* to the calling of an apostle, prophet, evangelist, pastor and/or teacher, please realize that callings are not *equivalent*. A professional clergy is given, as gifts, to equip God's people for works of service, so that the body of Christ may be built up (Eph. 4:11).

[46] *Christians at Work, Examining the Intersection of Calling & Career,* 50.

students, etc.[47] Integrators, according to Barna researchers, are 28% of the Christian workforce.

"Onlookers"—believers passively inclined towards integrating their faith and work, but are not actively doing so, are 38% and "Compartmentalizers," Christians with no inclination towards merging their faith and work, are 34%.[48]

To live missionally in the workplace is to join faith, mission, and career together and to transform any vocation, e.g., welder, grocery clerk, lawyer, doctor, construction worker, truck driver, mechanic, police officer, politician, fireman, logger, custodian, teacher, waiter, engineer, corporate CEO, or small business proprietor—to include taverns or tattoo businesses—into a missional vocation.

TRANSITION: DISCIPLES MAKING DISCIPLES—STAGE 3

Vanderstelt describes the Third Stage of a disciple's missional awareness development, as **Conscious/Competent**.[49] Stage 3 is thoroughly committed to the practice of beliefs—*Missional awareness is developed through the repetition of mission.*

The space between the third and fourth phases of a disciple's missional awareness development involves liminal (disorienting, challenging, threatening) mission experiences—*This is how Jesus makes disciples.*

---

[47] Ibid., 48-49.
[48] Ibid., 50.
[49] Jeff Vanderstelt, *Building A Missional Community,* Part 1.

CHAPTER 4

MISSION, MISSION, MISSION—COUPLING MISSION AND LIMINALITY

STAGE 3: "MODELING"

Missional awareness is developed through the repetition of mission. [50]
"And she tips them over the edge and into the air.

For the first time, the eaglets feel the air flowing through their wings, it's a new sensation but as they look at the ground far below, they become fearful of falling to their death, but the mother, in the last moment, swoops down and catches them on her back. And she returns them to what is left of the nest.

---

[50] Jeff Vanderstelt describes this phase in the development of a disciple's missional awareness as: **"conscious/competent."** Jeff Vanderstelt. *Building A Missional Community*, Part 1.

> *This painful, scary process is repeated until the eaglets learn to fly and then, a whole new world opens up to them…"*

As the mother eagle models flight for her young eaglets, the Apostle said to a first century Greek church, "Follow my example, as I follow the example of Christ" (1 Cor. 11:1) —*Paul modeled the life of a missional-driven disciple for the Corinthians.* Because he was in relationship with the Corinthians, they were able to see how the Apostle's theological teachings were *incarnated* in his life—*The relational dynamic of communitas is means for the missional congregation to organize around what the Spirit is doing.*

Forge International Network focuses their "energy on developing leadership that can understand the missional challenge and proactively develop strategies, approaches, and teams to be able to take the church onto new and uncharted ground."[51] On the Forge America website, the homepage proclaims: "We Long to See the Reign of God Revealed In The Everyday Spaces Of Life." [52]

Critical to Forge America's vision is the accessing of the works God "prepared in advance" for believers to do. Accessing the "good works" prepared by God involves an "Action-Reflection Learning Model."[53] This model is critical to Forge America's vision. Allan Hirsch explains that disciplemaking

---

[51] In 1996, The Forge Mission Training Network was founded in Australia by Alan and Deb Hirsch along with Michael Frost. Through a partnership with a missional training network in Canada, Forge expanded beyond Australia. The Forge Mission Training Network presently includes the United States, Russia, Scotland, England and Wales. Forge International Website http://www.forgeinternational.com/about#our-story downloaded, 07/15/2019.

[52] Forge America, http://www.forgeamerica.com/. Downloaded: 07/15/2019.

[53] Forge America Training Manual, Section 2, "The Local Forge Hub," 16, http://www.forgeamerica.com/, Downloaded: 07/12/2019.

is necessarily in the context of mission—This is how Jesus does discipleship, "... he organizes it around mission."[54]

Hirsch adds that immediately following the calling of his disciples, Jesus takes them on an "adventurous journey of mission, ministry, and learning. Straightaway they are involved in proclaiming the kingdom of God, serving the poor, healing, and casting out demons."[55]

In a missional congregation, discipleship begins in the life of the new convert by requiring them to participate in mission—"... mission is the catalyzing principle of discipleship."[56] Mission, as a "catalyzing principle," is most effectively done in a liminal context, that is, a context wherein the believer is "at risk" or out of "their comfort zone;" this is a situation in which they are "most inclined to learn."[57]

Luke 10:1-21 is an example of how mission is a catalyzing principle for the "triggering"[58] of the works God prepared in advance for us to do (Cf. Eph. 2:10). In verse 1, Jesus sends his disciples: *"After this the Lord appointed seventy-two others and sent them two by two ahead of him to every town and place where he was about to go."* (The Latinized form of "send" is *missio*).

What is the symbolic meaning of seventy-two disciples sent? In Genesis 10, there is a "table of nations," seventy-two nations are listed. This is sym-

---

[54] Allan Hirsch. *The Forgotten Ways*, 120.
[55] Ibid.
[56] Ibid.
[57] Forge America Training Manual, Section 2, "The Local Forge Hub," 16.
[58] Allan Hirsch. *The Forgotten Ways*. 22.

bolic of the restoration of the full-thrust of the Abrahamic Covenant—"*all the peoples on earth will be blessed through you,*" (Gen. 12:3b).[59]

MISSIO DEI—"GOD'S MISSION"

In Luke's Gospel, Jesus tells his disciples what their message is to be, "The kingdom of God has come near to you," (10:9)—The disciples' message is to announce the Gospel. In the first century context, "Gospel" referred to "an objective history changing event,"[60] that is about to take place!

The disciples are given "power and authority" to cast out demons and heal people, (Luke 9:1). This is what Jesus has been doing, following his announcement that the kingdom of God is "at hand," that is, the kingdom of God is breaking into history (cf. Matt. 4:17). Setting the demonically oppressed free is symbolic of an even greater reality; Jesus has come to liberate human souls from ultimate enslavement. And Jesus' healing of the crippled, blind, and deaf is symbolic of the greater reality that Jesus not only mends human bodies, but he is restoring the social fabric of the world—He is the source of new creation! (cf. Matt. 4:23; Rev. 21:5).

Jesus is *sending* his disciples on *His mission*, not their mission. "*Missio Dei*" (Latin) is "God's mission;" the disciples are to join God on His mission. And therefore, whoever, "… listens to you," Jesus said, "listens to me;" and "whoever rejects you rejects me; but whoever rejects me rejects him who sent me," 10:16. A most profound truth is spoken by Jesus: Anyone who refuses to hear the message of the Gospel—the announcement that

---

[59] The restoration of the full thrust of the Abrahamic Covenant is subsumed in the Cross of Christ and the Great Commission. The Abrahamic Covenant and its relation to the Great Commission is developed in Chapter 5, "A Royal Priesthood."
[60] Forge America Training Manual, 16.

the kingdom of God is breaking into world history—will be left behind.[61] The Gospel is not merely the best option, it is the *only* option for humankind (cf. Acts 4:12).

Inherent in the Gospel is world transformation. *Everything* —human lives, societies, cultures, nations, and the world is about to be transformed—"… the life of heaven, which had seemed so distant and unreal, is in the process of coming true on earth."[62]

Here, in Luke 10:1-16, the disciples are exposed to (made aware of), "God's mission" —The unique, unparalleled, history changing event of the ages; an event that transcends all ages for it was accomplished "before the creation of the world" (Eph. 1:4) and endures throughout eternity (Rev. 7:9-10). And please observe, the mission Jesus sent his disciples on was a liminal experience—the disciples endured severe rejection (their rejection was compared with Christ's rejection), intense spiritual warfare and, by implication, exhausting ministry. All of this was new to them, and no doubt, they were tested in extreme ways but, they experienced the presence of God in mightier ways—they were given "power and authority"!

And consequently, the disciples' joy, upon returning from their experience of joining God on "His Mission," was understandable (10:17) but it was necessary for Jesus to correct the peculiar *motivation* behind their rejoicing (10:18-20).

Jesus begins his correction of the disciples' motivation for rejoicing by saying, "I saw Satan fall like lightening from heaven"—For Jesus, this was a way of informing his disciples that he is their Source of power and triumph over evil, but to mortal ears this is awe-striking beyond description! What!? Before the creation of the world, Jesus defeated Satan in heaven! *By Jesus'*

---

[61] Ibid.
[62] N.T. Wright. *After You Believe, Why Christian Character Matters,* 105

authority, the disciples are experiencing in space-time-history what the pre-incarnate Word accomplished before space-time-history!

And following (10:20), Jesus exhorts his disciples, *"However, do not rejoice that the spirits submit to you ... "*—Jesus shifts the source of the disciples' motivation from *their* mission, and *personal achievement* to heaven (eternity) and what has *been* accomplished in their behalf, *"but rejoice that your names are written in heaven,"* (10:21).[63] God's authority and mission are in view, and after joining God on His mission, they are to rejoice in what God has prepared for them to do before the creation of the cosmos! The lordship of Jesus Christ is the authority over the mission the disciples are called to obediently carry out—*"New Testament theology is essentially missionary theology."*[64]

Christopher Wright stresses that New Testament revelation, "... came into being as the result of a two-part mission": (1) God the Father sent God the Son, Jesus Christ, into the world to inaugurate his kingdom with the blessings it brings to people and to call people to respond to it, and (2) the mission of his followers to continue his work by proclaiming him as Lord and Savior and calling people to faith is an ongoing commitment to him, and as a result, his church grows.[65]

God will use pain, turmoil, and loss as reliable teachers—*"When the pain becomes acute, we become open to change."* Seasoned missional practitioners (post-stage four regarding missional awareness) are acutely aware of God's use of his "reliable teachers" and they, therefore, take up the apostolic

---

[63] Culturally, for your name to be "written" (this is, of course, an age with no printing presses) meant that you were a nobleman, you were royalty—And so, Jesus has called *all* Christians "*to a royal priesthood*" (1 Pet. 2:9a). "A Royal Priesthood," both biblically and historically, will be discussed in Chapter 5, "Incarnational Mission."
[64] Christopher Wright. *The Mission of God*, 50.
[65] Ibid.

role in the missional church of making disciples beginning with luminally-laden mission.

POSTSCRIPT: COUPLING LIMINAL AND MISSION IN THE BOOK OF ACTS

Please observe the pattern of the coupling of liminal and mission throughout Acts—And reflect on how communitas, deeply committed, spiritual relationships, is forged by the fires of liminality, that is, experiences that are threatening, and oftentimes disorienting and consequently, test the disciples' resolve. The coupling of mission and liminal is catalytic to making disciples who then, through obedience to Jesus' Great Commission, make disciples. [66]

In Acts 4, the priests and the captain of the temple guard and the Sadducees arrested Peter and John because they were publicly proclaiming the resurrection and healing the infirmed in the name of Jesus Christ (4:1-2). Peter and John were brought before the Sanhedrin to be questioned by them. But Peter, "filled with the Holy Spirit," boldly defended the healing of the lame man (3:2-10) and he then proclaimed the risen Lord, Jesus Christ to all who were present.

Following their release, Peter and John returned to the fledgling church and reported to them all what the chief priests and elders had said to them. The church then prayed, acknowledging God's power and providence, and called on him to be with them and empower them to do his will, "Now, Lord, consider their threats and enable your servants to speak your word with great boldness. Stretch out your hand to heal and perform signs and wonders through the name of your holy servant Jesus" (Acts 4:3-31).

Acts 4:32-37 is a picture of true Christian community (communitas): "All the believers were one in heart and mind" … "With great power the

---

[66] Allan Hirsch. *Forgotten Ways*. 120.

apostles continued to testify to the resurrection of the Lord Jesus. And God's grace was so powerfully at work in them all that there were no needy persons among them."

In Acts 5:1-11, "Great fear seized the whole church and all who heard about these events" is a reference to Ananias and his wife, Sapphira, dying in the presence of Peter because they had lied to the Holy Spirit regarding money, they coveted for themselves from the sale of their property.

But following (Acts 5:12-16) the apostles perform signs and wonders among the believers who met together in Solomon's Colonnade to worship Jesus—"more and more men and women believed in the Lord and were added to their number." People brought the sick into the streets so that Peter's shadow might fall on some and they would be healed, and crowds of people gathered, bringing their sick and those tormented by malignant spirits for them to be healed and set free.

Acts 5:17 records the arrest and imprisonment of the apostles by the high priest because of their public ministry. During the night, while the jailed apostles were waiting to be interrogated by the high priest and his associates, an angel of the Lord opened the doors of the jail and set them free. When the Sanhedrin came together the following morning, they sent for the apostles but upon arriving at the jail, the officers did not find them there.

Someone came to the elders and announced that the apostles were in the temple courts teaching the people. The apostles were then brought before the Sanhedrin. The Sanhedrin vainly attempted to silence the apostles but after the apostles told them that God had raised Jesus Christ from the dead, the One whom they crucified, the disciples swore to obey God instead of them.

The vindictive plans of the Sanhedrin to kill Peter and the other apostles were placed on hold following Gamaliel's counsel to leave the apostles alone and wait and see if their purpose is from God, or not, based on its success or failure. In this way, the Sanhedrin will avoid "fighting against God."

Gamaliel's advice persuaded the Sanhedrin; and the apostles, following their flogging, were ordered not to speak in Jesus' name and they were released. "The apostles left the Sanhedrin rejoicing because they had been counted worthy of suffering for the Name."

Acts 6 speaks of the great increase of followers of Jesus and the apostolic appointment of seven men, full of the Spirit and wisdom, to serve as deacons by waiting on tables, that is, meeting the needs of the people while the apostles proclaimed the Gospel—*As the church was growing, communitas was deepening and flourishing in the church, and the church began organizing around what the Spirit was doing.*

Among the men chosen was Stephen, "a man full of God's grace and power," who performed "great wonders and signs among the people." Soon, a liminal situation erupted, members of the Synagogue of the Freedman (as they were so-called), Jews of Cyrene and Alexandria as well as the provinces of Cilicia and Asia began arguing with Stephen. But they were unable to contend with the wisdom the Holy Spirit gave to Stephen and so, they began to falsely accuse him claiming that he had spoken blasphemous words against Moses and God.

Soon, they stirred up both the people and their leaders, the elders, and the teachers of the law. Stephen was seized and brought before the Sanhedrin. Many testified falsely against him, and the high priest asked Stephen if the charges against him were true (Acts 7:1). Stephen responded by proclaiming the Gospel, beginning with God's covenant with Abraham, followed by an historical account of God's providential acts in the lives of Isaac, Jacob, Joseph, Moses, David, and Solomon—a powerful proclamation of God's covenantal purposes on behalf of his people and the world!

Stephen's defense exposed the hypocrisy of the "stiff-necked," "uncircumcised of heart" members of the Sanhedrin. The Sanhedrin broke out in a frenzy; they rushed Stephen, and drug him outside of the city and stoned him to death. Stephen, however, did not stop testifying to the glory of Jesus until his last breath—"He then fell on his knees and cried out, 'Lord, do not hold this sin against them.' When he said this, he fell asleep" (Acts 7:60).

Chapter 8 begins, "And Saul approved of their killing him." But Acts 9 begins with the conversion of Saul—*The Gospel is about to spread throughout the Roman empire and the known world!* The life of the Apostle Paul is marked by a rapid pace of liminal/communitas events from his blindness following his Damascus road conversion and the restoring of his sight following Ananias' prayer to confronting a Jewish sorcerer and false prophet (Acts 13:6) to being stoned in Lystra (Acts 14:19) to beatings and imprisonments, first in Philippi (Acts 16:22-24); to a riot threatening his life (Acts 17:5) to extremely fearful circumstances in Corinth (18:9), and followed by another life-threatening riot (19:23-24). In Jerusalem, Paul's life is threatened, and he is again arrested (21:32-33) and in 27:27-44, he is shipwrecked and stranded in the sea.

However, in contrast to his many liminal experiences, Paul experiences the power of God and occasions of communitas among new believers. In Acts 16:6, Paul receives a vision to go to Macedonia and in 16:11, the first European convert, Lydia, becomes a disciple (16:14-15); in16:25, Paul is delivered from imprisonment because of an earthquake (16:25), and in 17:10-11, the Apostle preaches to lovers of Scripture in Berea; Paul is comforted by the Lord in 18:9-10, and in 19:4-7, Paul experiences an outpouring of God's Spirit.

The Apostle engages in a series of defenses of the Gospel, first, before the Athenians, 17:16-34; then in 24:22-26, 25:8-12, and 25:23-26:32, Paul defends the "faith once delivered" before Felix, Festus, and King Agrippa. In Acts 28:5-6, Paul experiences God's healing after being bitten by a poisonous snake and in 28:16-31, Paul arrives in Rome and though a prisoner, the Apostle "proclaimed the kingdom of God and taught about the Lord Jesus Christ—with all boldness and without hindrance!" (28:16-31).

TRANSITION: MAKING DISCIPLES—STAGE 4

Vanderstelt describes the Fourth Stage of a disciple's missional awareness development, as **Unconscious/Competent.**[67] The believer's part in the Jesus story is dynamically realized through their introduction to joining God on his mission (*Missio Dei*) and the ancient/future reality that God calls *all* believers to "a royal priesthood" (1 Pet. 2:5; 9) through whom He engages the world.

---

[67] Jeff Vanderstelt, *Building A Missional Community*, Part 1.

CHAPTER 5

INCARNATIONAL MISSION

STAGE 4: SOARING "IN THE ZONE"

Jeff Vanderstelt emphasizes "muscle memory" regarding phase four—"*You don't think about doing it.*" [68]

In Stage 4 of disciples making disciples, "*... the mother has used pain, fear, and modeling to transform fearful, nest bound eaglets into soaring young eagles.*"

Regarding the phenomenal performances of great athletes, sports analysts will sometimes say, "That guy is unconscious!"[69] Michael Jordon, when in "the zone," (a synonym for "unconscious") was a step ahead of everyone else on the court; he would take-over the game and perform at a level that literally determined the game's outcome.

---

[68] Jeff Vanderstelt describes this phase in the development of a disciple's missional awareness as: "**unconscious/competent**." Jeff Vanderstelt, *Building A Missional Community*, Part 1.

[69] Ibid.

What required thoughtful processes in the third phase, is now in the "muscle memory" of the experienced missional-driven believer[70]—*The mother has used pain, fear, and modeling to transform fearful, nest bound eaglets into soaring young eagles.*

The believer acts in very competent, missional-driven ways—*The actions of the missional congregation and/or the individual missional practitioner are not at the forefront of their thinking, rather, they have discovered (better, "caught"), following repeated missions, that missional is in their spiritual DNA.*

How do you daily "soar in the zone"? By daily joining Jesus on His mission—Like Dave Bennett, the "Market-Place Pastor," Matt Haynes, the owner of Filament Tattoo Company, the Bar Stool Pastor, Jeff Hathcock, and "Vic" the Cop on a Mission, we must see our work as a calling, no less than we see our pastor's work as a calling. What, precisely, is your calling?

A ROYAL PRIESTHOOD

"But you are a chosen people, a royal priesthood, a holy nation, God's special possession, that you may declare the praises of him who called you out of darkness into his wonderful light"—1 Peter 2:9.

In Genesis 12:1-3, God sovereignly calls Abram into covenant relationship: *The* LORD *had said to Abram, "Go from your country, your people and your father's household to the land I will show you. ² "I will make you into a great nation, and I will bless you; I will make your name great, and you will be a blessing. ³ I will bless those who bless you, and whoever curses you I will curse; and all peoples on earth will be blessed through you."*

The primary purpose of Abram's election (calling) was the reversal of the effects of the Fall of humanity (Gen. 3:1-21) —The … "'curse' from

---

[70] Ibid.

Adam, through Cain, through the Flood to Babel, begins to be reversed when God calls Abram and says, 'in you shall all the families of the earth be blessed.'"[71] In the Septuagint (the Greek translation of Genesis 12:3[72]) the verb—*be blessed*—is passive.[73] The passive, "be blessed,"[74] defines Abraham's and his descendants' mission to "all the families of the earth."[75]

God's blessing of Abraham with a "name" and making him the father of a great nation was for the sake of Abraham blessing "all peoples on earth" (Gen. 12:3). And consequently, Israel was chosen from its origins through Abraham's election, for a missional mandate to "all peoples on earth"—"All that Israel was or was supposed to be—all that Yahweh their God did in

---

[71] N.T. Wright. *The New Testament and the People of God.* 262.
[72] The Septuagint is from 250-225 B.C. The Old Testament was translated from Hebrew to Greek for the purpose of Greek-speaking Jewish people's ability to read and understand the Old Testament Scriptures. This translation was accomplished by 70 Jewish scholars and therefore, the Septuagint is often designated by the Roman numeral LXX.
[73] Walter C. Kaiser, Jr. "The Great Commission in the Old Testament," page 4 of 7 pages. file:///C:/Users/theWr/AppData/Local/Packages/Microsoft.MicrosoftEdge_8wekyb3d8bbwe/TempState/Downloads/01_Kaiser%20(1).pdf Downloaded: 04/10/019
[74] M. Daniel Carroll R, notes: "… the patriarchs and their descendants are to be channels of blessing to others, as well as a paradigm of faith to which others might aspire. One can opt for the passive here in 12:1-3 and still appreciate the appropriateness of the reflexive as an extension of the mission." *Blessing the Nations: Toward a Biblical Theology of Mission from Genesis. Bulletin for Biblical Research 10.1 (2000) 17-34.* Page 24 of 34 pages. file:///C:/Users/theWr/AppData/Local/Packages/Microsoft.MicrosoftEdge_8wekyb3d8bbwe/TempState/Downloads/BBR_2000_a_02_Carroll_BlessingTheNations%20(1).pdf. Downloaded: 04/10/2019.
[75] Ibid. Page 21 of 34 pages.

them, for them, and through them—was ultimately linked to this wider purpose of God for the nations."[76]

The structure of Genesis 12:1-3 places stress on the notion that for God's people to be a blessing (vv. 2b-3), they must first receive blessing from God (vv. 1-2a).[77] God made available the blessing he intended for Abram by first commissioning him to "Go"—*Mission, and consequent blessing, flows from God.*

Towards the ultimate fulfillment of the Abrahamic covenant, that is, the blessing of all people and nations on earth (cf. Gen 12:3), God's intended "self-understanding" for Israel is explicit in His blessing of them. Through Moses, God made this clear, *"… Now if you obey me fully and keep my covenant, then out of all nations you will be my treasured possession. Although the whole earth is mine, you will be for me a kingdom of priests and a holy nation. These are the words you are to speak to the Israelites"* (Ex. 19:5-6).

God's missional intention for Israel was for every Israelite to be a priest. "For whom were all the Israelites to act as priests?" Walter Kaiser answers his own inquiry, "… they were to be priests for all the nations of the earth!"[78]—*As Israel was blessed, they were to bless other nations.* But Israel refused to obey God, and consequently, the lone tribe of Levi was appointed to serve as priests on behalf of the nation.[79]

---

[76] Christopher J. H. Wright. "Truth with a Mission: Reading All Scripture Missiologically." file:///C:/Users/theWr/AppData/Local/Packages/Microsoft.MicrosoftEdge_8wekyb3d8bbwe/TempState/Downloads/2_sbjt-v15-n2_wright%20(1).pdf Page 9 of 15 pages. Downloaded 04/13/2019

[77] M. Daniel Carroll R., *Blessing the Nations: Toward a Biblical Theology of Mission from Genesis.* Page 23 of 34 pages.

[78] Walter Kaiser. "The Great Commission in the Old Testament," page 4 of 7 pages.

[79] Ibid.

The purpose of Israel's election "was never merely an election to privilege: foremost of all it was an election to service—and that service was a world mission service—to share the blessing …"[80] with all peoples on earth (cf. Gen. 12:3). Although Abraham's descendants were blessed, they refused to be a blessing—they refused to be priests and make intercession between God and other nations. Israel failed God's missional purpose to be His witnesses (Isa. 43:10-12).

THE RENEWAL AND RESTORATION OF THE COVENANT

Yahweh has returned to renew and restore His covenant with Israel, in and through His Servant, the Messiah (cf. Isa. 52:13-15; 53). God's wrath, because of Israel's sins, has been averted through Messiah's death. But Yahweh has not only returned to renew and restore his covenant with Israel, but all nations: *"Scripture foresaw that God would justify the Gentiles by faith and announced the gospel in advance to Abraham: 'All nations will be blessed through you"* (Gal. 3:8). But Abraham's descendants, "all nations," have not been faithful to the covenant (cf. Romans 3:9-20; 23). How then is the Covenant renewed for Israel and restored for all nations?

On a Friday, late afternoon, God in Christ, made Himself, our Substitute: [13] *"Christ redeemed us from the curse of the law by becoming a curse for us, for it is written: 'Cursed is everyone who is hung on a tree.'* [14] *He redeemed us in order that the blessing given to Abraham might come to the Gentiles through Christ Jesus, so that by faith we might receive the promise of the Spirit"* (Gal. 3:13-14).

Jesus Christ is our *substitute* and through the blood of the Cross, the curse is broken—the seed of the woman has crushed the head of the serpent (Gen. 3:15)! And God's salvation is now a present reality for "all

---

[80] Ibid.

nations"[81]—*The original thrust of the covenant has been restored through the Cross!*[82] And now, Jews and Gentiles together are Abraham's seed through faith in Jesus (Gal. 3:29).

Abraham's seed, the recipients of "every spiritual blessing in Christ" (Eph. 1:3), are commissioned by Jesus Christ to "... *go and make disciples of all nations, baptizing them in the name of the Father and of the Son and of the Holy Spirit, and teaching them to obey everything I have commanded you. And surely, I am with you always, to the very end of the age*" (Mt. 28:19-20).

Towards the fulfillment of the Great Commission, Jesus' restoration of the full thrust of the Abrahamic Covenant includes God's original missional intention for Israel—"*Although the whole earth is mine, you will be for me a kingdom of priests and a holy nation*" (Ex. 19:5-6; cf. Gen. 12:3).

The "priesthood of all believers" was one of three dynamic motivations for the Protestant Reformation. Two of the three motivations, *Sola Scriptura,* the sole authority of holy Scripture, and *Sola Fide,* justification by "faith alone," are universally known among Protestant Christians.

But the third preeminent doctrine behind the Reformation, the "priesthood of all believers," has been virtually ignored and consequently, disobeyed by the church universal.

THE PRIESTHOOD OF ALL BELIEVERS

Exodus 19:5-6, quoted above, clearly tells us that Israel, as a nation, was to be "a priestly kingdom," "a royal priesthood." Exodus 19:5-6 provides

---

[81] Ps. 47:9; Isa 19:19-25; 56:3-8; 66:19-21; Zech. 2:10-11; Amos 9:11-12.
[82] Yahweh has returned in the person of Jesus of Nazareth to renew his covenant with Israel. See Isaiah: 49:8-26; 54:9-17; 56; 62:10-11; 63:1, 3,5,9; 64:1.

theological foundation for 1 Pet 2:5, 9 and Rev 1:6 and 5:10—The New Testament doctrine of "the priesthood of all believers."[83]

The kingdom of God is "a priestly kingdom"—1 Peter 2:5 says to *all* believers that "you also, like living stones, are being built into a spiritual house to be a holy priesthood, offering spiritual sacrifices acceptable to God through Jesus Christ." And 1 Peter 2:9 continues, "… you are a chosen people, a royal priesthood" called to intercede between God and sinful humanity.

N. T. Wright develops the intercessory role of a priest (every believer) by asserting that the church is called, "to discern where in your discipline the human project is showing signs of exile and humbly and boldly to act symbolically in ways that declare that the powers have been defeated, that the kingdom has come in Jesus the Jewish Messiah, that the new way of being human has been unveiled, and to be prepared to tell the story that explains what these symbols are all about."[84]

The "offering of spiritual sacrifices" (1 Peter 2:5) focuses on the "good works God has prepared in advance," and, also, the "masks of God." In his exposition of Psalm 147, the Reformer, Martin Luther (1483-1546), spoke of the "masks of God" to describe how God works through people in their vocation, that is, their calling to the work God has created them to do, e.g., construction worker, custodian, teacher, lawyer, physician, chef, banker, police officer, farmer, truck driver, waitress, logger, etc. (Eph. 2:10).[85]

For example, in Psalm 147, God's Word says, [13] "He strengthens the bars of your gates and blesses your people within you. [14] He grants peace to

---

[83] Walter Kaiser. "The Great Commission in the Old Testament," 4.
[84] Wright, The Challenge of Jesus, 187.
[85] "Luther on God's "Masks,'" Posted August 29, 2012, The Rev 2011 in Church History, Providence, Reformed Piety & Christian Nurture. https://christcovenantopc.wordpress.com/2012/08/29/luther-on-gods-masks/. Downloaded: 12/12/2019

your borders and satisfies you with the finest of wheat." Through police officers, God provides peace and safety to cities and rural towns (v. 13), through the armed forces, God brings "peace to your borders" and through restaurant waiters and waitresses, chefs, delivery men, wholesalers, workers in food-processing factories, butchers, farmers, ranchers, "and everyone else in the economic food chain," God gives me, "this day my daily bread." [86]

Now, the believer is distinguished from the unbeliever by their awareness of God's presence in their lives, and therefore, their faith, specifically regarding their calling, that is, their vocation. By joining Jesus on His mission and making our vocation—"whether in the fields, in the garden, in the city, in the house, in war, or in government"[87]—a means for the works God has prepared for us to do before the creation of the world (cf. Eph. 2:10), a Christian's vocation is transformed into a missional vocation, and we then perform in a priestly role. That is, God works through us to not only serve the material needs of others, but also the emotional and spiritual needs of those in exile.

In our priestly role, the church unveils "the new way of being human," to people "showing signs of exile"—broken, lost people, alienated from God and therefore, without Christ and without hope. Gene Veith observes that as "masks of God, even when we do not realize it, it is also true that God is masked in our neighbor. Particularly when our neighbor is in need—when he or she is sick, hungry, thirsty, naked, a prisoner, a stranger—Christ Himself is hidden. 'Inasmuch as ye have done it unto one of the least of

---

[86] Dr. Gene Edward Veith, Director of the Cranach Institute. "Masks of God." Downloaded 12/12/2019. http://mothersarehome.blogspot.com/2011/12/masks-of-god.html.

[87] J.D. Greear, pastor, The Summit Church, Raleigh-Durham, NC.
https://jdgreear.com/blog/martin-luther-on-gods-masks/. Downloaded: 12/12/2019.

these my brethren,' the Lord says, 'ye have done it unto me' (Matt. 25:40). In serving our neighbors, we end up serving Christ after all."[88]

And we are to "act symbolically," that is, we are to create environments for the kingdom of God to be made tangible (to be made real) for different people-groups, e.g., inner-city multi-housing residents, the homeless, addicts, prostitutes—whomever is your neighbor, in preparation for them to hear the Gospel.

Summarily, a member of the priesthood of all believers is to listen "to … needs …, expressing care and concern, offering prayer and bringing the God dimension to bear into a myriad of human situations …."[89] Obedience to the *Missio Dei*—"God's mission"—involves *every* disciple's divine *calling* to "a royal priesthood" so that believers "may declare the praises of him who called you [us] out of darkness into his wonderful light" (1 Pet. 2:5; 9; Rev. 1:6).

THE PRIESTHOOD OF ALL BELIEVERS & THE GREAT COMMISSION

In his "Open Letter to the Christian Nobility of the German Nation Concerning the Reform of the Christian Estate (1520),"[90] although Luther does not explicitly speak of a "sacred/secular divide" (*et. al.* Chapter 2) a similar, present disposition prompted the Reformer to condemn the notion that the work of the so-called layperson is inferior to the work of the clergy (e.g., priest or bishop): "It is pure invention that pope, bishops, priests,

---

[88] Ibid.
[89] Martin Robinson & Dwight Smith. *Invading Secular Space,* 121.
[90] Adapted from the translation of C. M. Jacobs (*Works of Luther,* Philadelphia: A. J. Holman Company, 1915*),* found online at: http://www.iclnet.org/pub/resources/text/wittenberg/luther/web/nblty-03.html.

and monks are to be called the 'spiritual estate'; princes, lords, artisans, and farmers the 'temporal estate.'"

Luther continues, "... that all Christians are truly of the 'spiritual estate,' and there is among them no difference at all but that of office, as Paul says in I Corinthians 12:12, "We are all one body, yet every member has its own work, where by it serves every other, all because we have one baptism, one Gospel, one faith, and are all alike Christians; for baptism, Gospel and faith alone make us 'spiritual' and a Christian people."[91]

And finally, Luther stresses, "Through baptism all of us are consecrated[92] to the priesthood, as St. Peter says in, I Peter 2:9, 'Ye are a royal priesthood, a priestly kingdom,' and the book of Revelation says, Rev. 5:10: 'Thou hast made us by Thy blood to be priests and kings.'"[93]

Therefore, concludes, Luther, "... the plowboy and the milkmaid could do priestly work. In fact, their plowing and milking *was* priestly work. So, there was no hierarchy where the priesthood was a 'vocation' and milking the cow was not. Both were tasks that God called his followers to do, each according to their gifts."[94]

We all have our "own work, whereby it serves every other," that is, every believer's vocation, e.g., waitress, mechanic, welder, teacher, construction, custodian, farmer, eco-cardiogram tech, grocery clerk, lawyer, nurse, bank teller, business owner, truck driver, police officer, soldier, airman, sailor, writer, musician, artist, etc., is to be coupled with their "consecration to

---

[91] Ibid., 1-2.
[92] "Consecrated" means we are set apart for the holy work Jesus Christ has commissioned us to do.
[93] Ibid., 2.
[94] Art Lindsey, Institute for Faith, Work & Economics. "The Priesthood of all Believers."https://tifwe.org/resource/the-priesthood-of-all-believers/Downloaded, 07/06/2019, 1 of 6.

the priesthood," or to put it another way, every working person's vocation is coupled with their call to be like God and therefore, to be missional.

The gifts, skills and talents God has blessed us with are *means* for God to do the "good works" He has prepared for us to do "in advance" in service to every other person. In this way, observes Luther, "many kinds of work may be done for the bodily and spiritual welfare of the community, even as all the members of the body serve one another."[95]

Through the "priesthood of all believers," every believer throughout the earth purposefully serving one person at a time, is enabled by the Holy Spirit to provide for the physical, social, and spiritual needs of the community and therein, he/she is making "disciples of all nations" (Matt. 28:18-20).

Paul affirmed that Genesis 12:3—"All nations will be blessed through you," was "the gospel in advance" (Gal. 3:8). Believers obedient to their calling to be "a royal priesthood," a mediator between God's blessing and the spiritually exiled world because of sin, will, in eternity, see the fulfillment of the renewed Abrahamic covenant (*et.al.* The Great Commission): [9]"After this I looked, and there before me was a great multitude that no one could count, from every nation, tribe, people, and language, standing before the throne and before the Lamb. They were wearing white robes and were holding palm branches in their hands. [10]And they [the Redeemed from every nation] cried out in a loud voice: 'Salvation belongs to our God, who sits on the throne, and to the Lamb'" (Rev. 7:9-10).

Exodus 19:5-6 clearly tells us that Israel, as a nation, was to be "a priestly kingdom," "a royal priesthood." Exodus 19:5-6 provided theological foundation for 1 Pet 2:5, 9 and Rev 1:6, and 5:10, along with the Reformers, to announce the New Testament doctrine of "the priesthood of all believers."[96] What ancient Israel refused to do, the New Testament and the Reformers

---

[95] Ibid., 3.
[96] Walter Kaiser. "The Great Commission in the Old Testament," 4.

attempted to recover in the church—*In every walk of life, the priesthood of all believers is to be Christ's witnesses for all nations throughout the earth* (Matt. 28:18-20).

INCARNATIONAL MISSION

The recovery in the church of the ancient/future missional vocation of the priesthood of all believers is crucial to the church's commission from Christ to "… go and make disciples of all nations, baptizing them in the name of the Father and of the Son and of the Holy Spirit," (Matthew 28:19).

It follows from the Holy Spirit's omnipresence that the kingdom of God is present *everywhere*—There is no sacred/secular divide. The Spirit *sends* the church to a particular people group, district or location in a city or a geographical [ethnic] area in a state, province or nation to perform in a priestly role (1 Pet. 2:9)—*The missional congregation (or individual missional entrepreneur) occupies the space between humanity's alienation and the reality of the present kingdom of God*—Ministers of reconciliation (priests) are making the reality of the kingdom of God tangible [real] for unbelievers by creating spaces or environments for the power of the Gospel to bring new creation (2 Cor. 5:17-20).

Through their consecration into the Priesthood of all Believers, every believer, every day, is a vital gift and contributor to the achievement of the Great Commission—*Please observe that the coupling of the priesthood of all believers, and "masks of God" is what we refer to today as incarnational mission*—Incarnational Mission is, precisely, the priestly calling of every believer.[97]

---

[97] Incarnational mission is a pervasive undercurrent throughout Part 2, *Living Missionally Beyond Sunday, Missional Congregations and the Missio Dei.*

Like the mother eagle's persistence in sending her eaglets to flight, the more and more missional congregations engage liminal conditions by joining Jesus on his mission, the greater is the spiritual experience of communitas in the church, and the visible presence of the kingdom of God in host communities throughout the earth!

CHAPTER 6

LIVING MISSIONALLY BEYOND SUNDAY!

PRINCIPLES IN THE mDNA[98] OF MISSIONAL CONGREGATIONS

Matthew 28:18-20—¹⁸ Then Jesus came to them and said,[99] "All authority in heaven and on earth has been given to me"[100]— The predicate is clearly covenantal and Deuteronomic,[101] Jesus

---

[98] Allan Hirsch appends DNA with the *m* to simply differentiate *missional* DNA from biological life—"What DNA does for biological systems, mDNA does for ecclesial ones." *The Forgotten Ways*, 283.

[99] Christopher J.H. Wright: "The words of Jesus to his disciples in Matthew 28:18-20, the so-called Great Commission, could be seen as a christological mutation of the original Abrahamic commission—"Go… and be a blessing… and all nations on earth will be blessed through you." *The Mission of God, Unlocking the Bible's Grand Narrative*. 213.

[100] Re: Daniel 7:14, Following his ascension and enthronement with Yahweh, the Son of Man has received sovereign dominion—Jesus is Lord.

[101] Deuteronomy 4:39: "Acknowledge and take to heart this day that the Lord is God in heaven above and on the earth below. There is no other." See Christopher Wright. Ibid., 355.

is the Lord God Almighty. And therefore, disciples of Jesus are obedient to his command: ¹⁹ "Therefore go" (πορευθέντες, lit. "Having gone" [102]) or "as you go"[103]—*Wherever a missional practitioner is, they are always on mission*—[104] ¹⁹ᵇ "… and making disciples of all nations," [105] ¹⁹ᵇ "… baptizing them in the name of the Father and of the Son and of the Holy Spirit, ("The unity of being"[106]—The holy Trinity is three coequal, coeternal, and coexistent Persons working in perfect unity through the church and/or individual

---

[102] πορευθέντες ("go") is literally, *"Having gone."* Grammatically, this is a Greek aorist participle of attendant circumstances. C. Wright. *The Mission of God*. 35. Essentially, the participle of attendant circumstances involves the communication of an action coordinate with the finite verb. For a full and refined (scholarly) understanding of the participle of attendant, please see, Daniel Wallace. *Greek Grammar, Beyond the Basics: An Exegetical Syntax of the New Testament with Scripture, Subject and Greek Word Indexes*. Grand Rapids, MI.: Zondervan, 1996. 640. Scott Allan Gilbert discusses Wallace's grammatical analyses in his dissertation. "Go Make Disciples: Sermonic Application of the Imperative of the Great Commission." A Dissertation Presented to the Faculty of: The Southern Baptist Theological Seminary. In Partial Fulfillment of the Requirements for the Degree Doctor of Philosophy. December 2017.152.

[103] Christopher Wright. *The Mission of God*. (Mt. 28:18-20, author's translation). 354. The term translated "go" is "functioning as an adverbial participle indicating time that is contemporaneous," that is, "as you go" (See also footnote #107).

[104] Mike Graves and David M. May, Preaching Matthew: Interpretation and Proclamation (St. Louis: Chalice Press, 2007), 137. Gilbert adds: "Similarly, in his commentary for preachers and teachers, Myron Augsburger suggests the best translation is "while going in the world." Myron S. Augsburger, Matthew, The Communicator's Commentary (Waco, TX: Word Books, 1982), 330." This view of the participle asserts that disciplemaking occurs as disciples go through daily life.

[105] C. Wright. *The Mission of God*. "Jesus did not primarily command his disciples to go; he commanded them to make disciples." (See footnote #1 and the intersection of the Great Commandment and the Abrahamic Covenant.

[106] *Theological Dictionary of the New Testament*. Vol. V. 274.

missional-driven disciple[s] obedient to the *Missio Dei*).[107] The emphasis is on the union of the one baptized in the name of the One True God; [20] "…and teaching them to obey everything I have commanded you. And surely, I am with you always, to the very end of the age." Wright observes, "The covenant presence of God among his people in the Old Testament becomes the promised presence of Jesus among his disciples as they carry out the mission, he lays on them."[108]

LIVING MISSIONALLY BEYOND SUNDAY!

"All authority in heaven and on earth has been given to me"—Jesus is Lord. "Therefore, as you go, make disciples of all nations, baptizing them in the name of the Father and of the Son and of the Holy Spirit, and teaching them to obey everything I have commanded you. And all peoples on earth will be blessed through you—Surely, I am with you always to the very end of the age" (Matt. 28:18-20).

PRINCIPLES IN THE "mDNA" OF MISSIONAL CONGREGATIONS

A SUMMARY OUTLINE OF DISCIPLEMAKING

"Jesus is Lord and Ceasar is Not"

Principles inherent in missional congregations' "mDNA" empower them to obediently respond to Jesus Christ's command for disciples to make disciples of all nations:

---

[107] Re.: Kerry D. McRoberts. "The Holy Trinity" (Ch. 5). *Systematic Theology, Pentecostal Perspectives*. Stanley Horton, Editor. Springfield, MO.: Logion Press, 1994.

[108] C. Wright. *The Mission of God*. 355.

- **Jesus Christ is Lord:** *Obedience to the penultimate enterprise of missional congregations to make disciples follows their acknowledgement of the ultimate confessional principle—Jesus is Lord!*
- **Disciples Making Disciples:** Following water baptism, disciple-making continues by teaching disciples to be obedient to everything He has commanded—*A disciple obeys Jesus in all of life and teaches others to do likewise.*
- **Christ is with us always**—The calling of *all* believers to a royal priesthood involves our Savior's great faithfulness in coming alongside of us and working through us in the Spirit's power to make disciples of all nations (cf. Gen. 12:3b). *The task of disciplemaking is continual, "to the very end of the age" in missional congregations*

DISCIPLEMAKING—FIVE VITAL STAGES:[109]

STAGE #1: CHALLENGING "NEST-BOUND" BELIEVERS

"Nest-bound" believers resist joining God on His mission (*MissioDei*) —

These believers just "*don't know that they don't know*"—Jeff Vanderstelt.

"*But eagles were not born to live in a nest, they were born to fly, and the mother knows this. When the young eagles have grown feathers, the mother coaxes them to the top, to the edge of the nest to fly. The mother challenges her young to step out of the nest and fly, but they are afraid, and they resist.*"

---

[109] The five eagle images presented here, the "Nest-Bound Eagle," the "Vocational Eagle," the "Liminal Eagle," the "Soaring eagle," and the "Professor Eagle," are the creations of Vicki McRoberts, "Intrinsic Doodles Inc."

STAGE #1: PRINCIPLES IN THE mDNA OF MISSIONAL CONGREGATIONS

Reality is Coupled—cf. Genesis 1:1, 4, 10,13,14, and 27

- **The recoupling of "the heavens and the earth"** in the biblically transformed worldview of believers results in a post secular view of reality and consequent realization that: *"There are no unsacred places; there are only sacred places and desecrated places."*
- The objective of Stage #1 is to challenge the "nest-bound" believer to pivot his or her mindset from a "church-centric" perspective to an understanding that mission is Christo-centric—*The Missio Dei flows from the holy Trinity into the historical flow of everyday life and brings transformation to God's creation through his covenant people* (Gen. 12:3b; 1 Pet. 2:5, 9).

STAGE #2: *"BORN TO FLY"*—THE MISSIONAL VOCATION

"I realize I really don't know"—Jeff Vanderstelt.

"… eagles were not born to inhabit a nest, but to fly…"

STAGE #2: PRINCIPLES OF MISSIONAL CONGREGATIONS

"The only Christian work is good work well done"—Dorothy Sayers

- **Coupling Mission and Vocation:** For the disciple to abide in the ultimate purpose and passion of the daily reality of the *Missio Dei,* the creation ordinance of work must be coupled with mission—Believers must *transform* their vocation (calling) into a *missional vocation*.

- **Good Works Prepared in Advance:** *"... whoever believes in me will do the works I have been doing, and they will do even greater things than these, because I am going to the Father"*—John 14:12 (cf. Eph. 2:10, Lk. 4:16-17/Mt. 11:4-6; Rom. 12:3-8, 1 Cor. 12:1-11 and Eph. 4:2-9).

—STAGE #3: MISSION, MISSION, MISSION—AND "MODELING"

Missional awareness increases through the repetition of mission - Jeff Vanderstelt

"And she tips them over the edge and into the air.

For the first time, the eaglets feel the air flowing through their wings, it's a new sensation but as they look at the ground far below, they become fearful of falling to their death, but the mother, in the last moment, swoops down and catches them on her back. And she returns them to what is left of the nest.

This painful, terrifying process is repeated until the eaglets learn to fly and then, a whole new world opens up to them..."

STAGE #3: PRINCIPLES IN THE mDNA OF MISSIONAL CONGREGATIONS

Missional awareness is made evident through the repetition of mission—And ...

- **Modeling:** To the elders of the church at Ephesus, Paul said, "You know how I lived the whole time I was with you, from the first day

I came into the province of Asia" (Acts 20:18)—Paul modeled the whole Christian life to the believers in Ephesus (and wherever else he joined God's Mission). As Paul modeled the faith "once delivered" for ancient believers, seasoned missional practitioners are called to model the "good works God prepared in advance for us to do" for believers in missional congregations, especially in liminal conditions on mission.

- **Liminal:** In a particular scene in the "parable" of the Wizard of Oz, the wicked "Witch of the West" launches nasty, tormenting flying monkeys that attack Dorothy and her three companions, creating extremely difficult circumstances for them. However, the trials associated with the turmoil and chaos served to "trigger" the awareness of the Scarecrow, the Tin Man, and the Cowardly Lion that they already possessed the brain, the heart, and the courage they so desperately longed for.

And likewise, as a "catalyzing principle," [110] mission coupled with "liminal" conditions—an environment wherein the disciple is "at risk" or "out of their comfort zone"—invokes a deeply felt internalized awareness of God's mission and consistently serves to "trigger" the flow of the "good works God prepared in advance for us to do" through the "proactive"[111] missional- driven disciple. [112]

- **Communitas:** The relational dynamic of communitas is means for the missional church to organize around what the Spirit is doing— *Like the mother eagle's persistence in sending her eaglets to flight, the*

---

[110] Alan Hirsch. *The Forgotten Ways*, 120.
[111] Contrary to a passive posture, "proactive" involves the missionally driven believer actively meeting needs and witnessing for Christ and consequently, experiencing the power of the Spirit working the "good works God prepared in advance for us to do" through himself or herself.
[112] Allan Hirsch. *The Forgotten Ways*, 22.

more and more missional congregations engage liminal conditions by joining Jesus on his mission, the greater is the spiritual experience of communitas in the church, and the visible presence of the kingdom of God in host communities throughout the earth![113]

—STAGE 4: SOARING "IN THE ZONE"— INCARNATIONAL MISSION

Vanderstelt emphasizes "muscle memory" regarding phase four—*"You don't think about doing it"*—Jeff Vanderstelt.

"The mother has used pain, fear, and modeling to transform fearful, nest bound eaglets into soaring young eagles…"

STAGE #4: PRINCIPLES IN THE mDNA OF MISSIONAL CONGREGATIONS

Jesus used pain, fear, and modeling as catalysts to transform insecure followers into soaring missional-driven disciples (Lk. 10:1-21).[114]

- **A Priestly Kingdom:** Missional Congregations occupy the space between humanity's alienation and the reality of the present kingdom of God—Ministers of reconciliation (priests) are making the reality of the kingdom of God tangible [real] for unbelievers by

---

[113] See Allan Hirsch, *The Forgotten Ways*, Chapter 8, "Communitas *Not* Community," 217-241 for a full discussion of Communitas.

[114] Please see Ch.4: The Coupling of Liminal and Communitas in the Book of Acts. *The book of Acts, for example, demonstrates how consistently liminal experiences—threatening experiences in which malignant spiritual strongholds confront disciples—are followed by the blessedness of communitas, ever-increasing levels of relational commitment to one another among missionally-driven believers.*

creating spaces or environments for the power of the Gospel to bring new creation (2 Cor. 5:17-20/1 Pt. 2:5, 9).

- **Incarnational Mission:** *"And surely I am with you always…"*—In every walk of life, through incarnational mission (viz., the coupling of the Royal Priesthood of all Believers and the "masks of God"), the Holy Spirit comes alongside of believers, and He works through us to bless and make disciples of all nations (Gen. 12:3b/Matt. 28:20b).
- **Contextualization:** Joining the trinitarian God in what he is doing in the world, requires believers to read the cultural signs and always to be ready to adapt and connect the Gospel and missional praxis to changing cultural environments. Missional practitioners need to create environments that result in genuine identification with those in exile.

Paul's apostolic ministry was a model for contextualizing the Gospel (1 Cor. 9:19-23): By means of genuine identification with those in "exile," Paul was following his Lord's example—"Though I am free and belong to no one, I have made myself a slave to everyone …," 9:19. Paradoxically, Paul uses his freedom in Christ to become "a slave to everyone." Because Paul is Christ's slave, he is not owned (obligated) to/by any man—Paul's enslavement to man, was his choice, not any man's.

Regarding the Christian ethic, it is imperative to stress Paul's point: Freedom is not Paul's goal, but rather the salvation of others is.[115] Therefore, Paul chose to become a slave to men for the sake of winning "as many as possible," 9:19. Fee observes, "Free, in order to become slave to all—

---

[115] Gordon Fee. *The New International Commentary on the New Testament, The First Epistle to the Corinthians*, 426.

this is surely the ultimate expression of truly Christian, because it is truly Christlike, behavior."[116]

Jesus became a "slave" of all for the sake of *our freedom through his saving grace* (cf. Phil. 2:5-8; Gal. 4:4-5)[117] and consequently, Paul willingly conforms to the cultural expectations of whatever social context he is in for "the sake of the gospel," 9:23—"To the Jews," Paul "became like a Jew;" 9:20, "To those under the law," Paul "became like one under the law;" 9:20, "To those not having the law," Paul "became like one not having the law;" 9:21, "To the weak," Paul "became weak," 9:22. Paul's contextualization of the Gospel indicates that "… when he was among Jews, he was kosher; when he was among Gentiles, he was non-kosher—*precisely because, as with circumcision, neither mattered to God* (cf. 7:19; 8:8).[118]

Regarding Jews, in this context, they abstain from certain foods because they are "under the law," they are under religious obligation. And regarding Gentiles, Paul was not lawless, but he obeys the ethical imperatives of Christian faith now written on hearts of flesh (cf. Ezek. 36:26-27).[119] Paul was uncompromising concerning matters that affected the Gospel, regardless if they were theological or behavioral matters (e.g., 1 Cor. 1:18-25; 5:1-5, etc.), never-the-less, the saving power of the Gospel motivates him to "become all things to all people" in matters that do not count.[120] Regarding "the weak," Paul is probably referring to a social category of people.[121] Paul's argument, concerning his becoming "all things to all people," is purely, "for

---

[116] Ibid.
[117] Ibid.
[118] Ibid., 427.
[119] Ibid., 430.
[120] Ibid., 431.
[121] Ibid. 431

the sake of the gospel," 9:23—David Schmidgall succinctly sums up contextualization: *"What does the Good News look like here?"*[122]

STAGE #5: THEOLOGY, MISSION, AND COMMUNITY
APPENDIX 1: DISCIPLES MAKING DISCIPLES—"TEACHING THEM TO OBEY..."

Appendix 1 couples Part 1, "Disciples Making Disciples," and Part 2, *"Living Missionally Beyond Sunday!* Missional Congregations & The Missio Dei," of this book. In Stage 5, each of the first 4 Stages of disciplemaking is identified with select resources related to theology, mission, and community. Cohorts, led by a facilitator, gather to discuss selected readings under each of the first four phases of discipleship in Part 1 of this book—Stage 5 creates space for communitas through missional theological formation and *koinonia*.

PART 2: "LIVING MISSIONALLY BEYOND SUNDAY!"

Part 2, *Living Missionally Beyond Sunday!* Missional Congregations & The Missio Dei, begins with a missional reading of Acts 8:1-25 and the formulation of a Missional Theology around its nucleus, The *Missio Dei*. Following (Chapters 8-16), Pastors of missional congregations, directors of missional enterprises, and managers of "third places" are interviewed—*The stories of the 10 interviewees (+ my story) express the practices of missional enterprises in imaginatively, unique, and nuanced ways as they work out a missional theology.*

---

[122] David Schmidgall. National Community Church, Lincoln Theatre Campus Pastor. "Partnering in the Mission of Jesus." https://national.cc/media/disciple/partnering-in-the-mission-of-jesus. Downloaded: 09/24/2021.

Chapter 17, "Common & Unique Strands of Missional DNA" summarizes (and illustrates) both practices and principles of missional congregations, Christian organizations, and third places. And Appendix 1, "Disciples Making Disciples"—Stage 5: "Teaching Them To Obey"—Stage 5 creates space for communitas through missional theological formation and *koinonia*.

PART 2

LIVING MISSIONALLY BEYOND SUNDAY!

MISSIONAL CONGREGATIONS AND THE MISSIO DEI

CHAPTER 7

THE *MISSIO DEI* & A MISSIONAL THEOLOGY

"But you will receive power when the Holy Spirit comes on you; and you will be my witnesses in Jerusalem, and in all Judea and Samaria, and to the ends of the earth" (Acts 1:8).

Acts, chapter 8, begins by describing Saul's consenting of Stephen's martyrdom. A "great persecution" of the primitive church in Jerusalem then results in the scattering of Jesus' "witnesses" throughout "Judea and Samaria" (Acts 8:1).

The widespread persecution began with the Sadducees, but Stephen's death was directly at the hands of the Pharisees—Both parties then united in the "great persecution." And Saul soon becomes the leader of the widespread persecution (Acts 8:3).

Although it is a mystery why the Apostles were not directly attacked, nevertheless, God's missional ends prevail over the rage-driven persecution of Saul and the two parties of the Sanhedrin—The Lord uses the persecution of his church to *send* (the Greek term translated, "scatter" means *disperse*, "to sow in separate or scattered places"[123]) his disciples from Jerusalem to specific people groups, particularly, Samaria (Acts 8:4).[124] Jesus' disciples are to be "witnesses" (Acts 1:8)[125] of God's grace in Christ to a people who have been the objects of their racial hatred for centuries![126]

It is noteworthy that although Acts 1:5 speaks of Philip going "to a city in Samaria" and proclaiming, "the Messiah there," this is not a reference to the apostle, named Philip (Mk. 3:18), but rather a deacon (et.al., Acts 6:5).

Jesus' earlier ministry in Samaria was modeled for the disciples (John 4), though the disciples had been forbidden to go to Samaria. But the time is now right—The promise of the Father has clothed the church in power (Lk. 24:49/Acts 1:4-5; 2:1-4). And Jesus' disciples are sent (beginning with a deacon, not an apostle, and perhaps his daughters, Acts 21:8) to missionally engage Samaria.

Philip's proclamation of the Gospel was followed by two signs that point to the now present kingdom of God, the deliverance of people

---

[123] A.T. Robertson. *Word Pictures of the New Testament.* Vol. III, Acts. Grand Rapids, MI. Baker Book House, 1930. 102.

[124] Jesus told his disciples to remain in Jerusalem until after the "promise of the Father" came upon them (Acts 1:4; cf. Luke 24:49). But the disciples continued to remain in Jerusalem, after receiving the promise of the Father, instead of proclaiming the Gospel to other peoples (cf. Acts 1:8).

[125] The Greek term translated "witnesses" is *martures* from which comes our word, martyrs.

[126] The acrimony between Jews and Samaritans originated centuries before, during the disruption of the Hebrew monarchy following Solomon's death in 930 B.C. The Judeans regarded the Samaritans to be "racial and religious half-breeds" because these foreign settlers were planted in Samaria by the Assyrians to take the place of the upper classes of the land who were deported at the time of the fall of the northern kingdom of Israel (Cf. 2 Kings 17:24ff.; Ezra 4:2, 9f.). This period was from 721 – 705 B.C. during the reign of Sargon II, the Assyrian king). Despite the Samaritans turning from their pagan roots and embracing Judaism, the Jews continued to refuse to have anything to do with them, their hatred ran deep in their souls.

bound by malignant spirits and the healing of many who were "paralyzed" or "lame."[127] The awe-struck Samaritans "paid close attention" to Philip[128] (Acts 8:6-7).

The Samaritans had come under the spell of the occult power of a sorcerer, but the power working through Philip was greater than Simon Magus' power. And the Samaritans believed the Good News proclaimed by Philip and they were baptized (Acts 8:12).

Simon, the sorcerer, was "astonished by the great signs and miracles he saw," and he, "himself believed and was baptized" (Acts 8:13). But it is apparent that Simon's motives were self-serving, he wanted the power Philip had so that he could regain his power over the Samaritan people—"He was probably half victim of self-delusion, half conscious imposter" (Furneaux).[129]

Philip is joined by Peter and John (Acts 8:14)—Since "the apostles in Jerusalem heard that Samaria had accepted the word of God," they sensed a need to go to Samaria, perhaps they felt the need to sanction Philip's ministry among the Samaritans, particularly for the sake of the acceptance of Jewish Christians.

Because "the Holy Spirit had not yet come on any" of the Samaritans, Peter, and John "prayed for the new believers," so that they "might receive the Holy Spirit" (Acts 8:15-16). When Simon "saw that the Spirit was given at the laying on of the apostles' hands, he offered them money" (Acts 8:18). "When Simon saw," grammatically implies "that those who received

---

[127] Setting people free from torment by demonic spirits is a sign pointing to God's willingness to set all repentant people free from bondage to sin and healing points to God's ultimate intention to "make all things new" (Rev. 21:1-7).

[128] A.T. Robertson. *Word Pictures in the New Testament.* 103.

[129] Ibid. 105.

the gift of the Holy Spirit spoke with tongues."[130] Simon *saw* power given to others, and he is determined to purchase this authority for himself.

Peter confronts Simon's evil motives (Acts 8:20) but he still leaves room for the sorcerer to repent (Acts 8:22). As Peter and John returned to Jerusalem, they preached the Gospel in many Samaritan towns (Acts 8:25).

Acts 8:1-25 is a missional text, that is, it is a divinely inspired model of the *Missio Dei* and the corresponding missional practices of the Lord's earliest disciples on a liminally-ladened mission. *A missional reading/interpretation of Acts 8:1-25 is applied to biblically based practices essential for the formulation of a missional theology in the following:*

PRACTICES OF MISSIONAL CONGREGATIONS

"… you are a chosen people, a royal priesthood"—1 Peter 2:9

The restoration of the full thrust of the Abrahamic Covenant to the Gentile world has made *all* believers, Jew, and Gentile, male and female, a "kingdom of priests." And the Priesthood of *all* Believers is called to join God on his mission—*"and all peoples on earth will be blessed through you"* (Gen. 12:3b/Mt. 28:18-20).

MISSIONAL THEOLOGY

"As the Father has sent me, I am sending you"—John 20:21

A missional reading of the Bible, to include Acts 8:1-25, serves as basis for the formulation of a missional theology—*Missional theology defines missional congregations.* And therefore, a missional theology properly frames the practices of both missional congregations and individual missional practitioners. The *Missio Dei* —The Mission of God— is the nucleus of

---

[130] Ibid. 107. "When Simon saw"—participle, second aorist active of *horáō*.

a missional theology and consequently, it is the primary *cause* of missional congregations.

THE MISSIO DEI

> *"Our mission flows from and participates in the mission of God"*—Christopher Wright.[131]

The *Missio Dei* originates with God—The *Missio Dei* is a divine reality from which flows the space-time missions by which God engages and transforms the world through his covenant people. *The biblical view of the divine origins of the Missio Dei calls 21st Century disciples to observe that God created the church for mission, instead of mission for the church* (et. al. John 20:21b).

And consequently, God's Mission—*Missio Dei*—providentially preceded and sovereignly presided over the "great persecution" in ordinary space-time and history in Acts 8:1-3. That is, the "great persecution" of God's church was in the flow of the mission of God—*The "great persecution" was used by God towards his missional ends, the reign of Christ in the lives of a specific people group, the Samaritans* (Acts 8:4-5).

God's grand narrative (Biblical revelation) places redeemed humanity—from the beginning of creation and time until the return of Christ and a new heaven and a new earth—in the flow of the eternal reality of his mission. And thus, God's covenant people glorify God through their obedience to the *Missio Dei*—"Fundamentally, our mission (if it is biblically informed and validated) means our committed participation as God's people, at God's invitation and command, in God's own mission within the history of God's world for the redemption of God's creation."[132]

---

[131] Christopher J.H. Wright. *The Mission of God.* 23.
[132] Ibid., 22-23.

Towards the formulation of a missional theology, the *Missio Dei* is the nucleus around which space-time mission orbits—*Biblically based practices of missional congregations and individual missional entrepreneurs flow from God's mission*. The following practices of missional congregations are outstanding in a missional reading of the Bible, to include, Acts 8:1-25.

THE MISSIO DEI AND ITS MISSIONAL ORBIT

> *Mission... "arises from the heart of God himself and is communicated from his heart to ours. Mission is the global outreach of the global people of a global God"*—John Stott.[133]

MISSION

> *"And what does the Lord require of you? To act justly and love mercy and to walk humbly with your God"*—Micah 6:8.

Mission, in the context of a missional theology, "means the committed *participation* of God's people in the purposes of God for the redemption of the whole creation."[134] Mission is divinely distinguished as follows:

- Mission does not begin with God's elect, e.g., the patriarchs, the prophets, the apostles, the primitive or the modern church—*Mission is not in the flow of church tradition, but rather, its origins are divine, mission flows from the holy Trinity, the Father, the Son, and the Holy Spirit into world history and particular events* (e.g., Lk. 24:49/ Acts 1:4-5; Acts 1:8/2:1-4).

---

[133] John Stott. *The Contemporary Christian: Applying God's Word To Today's World.* Downers Grove, Ill.: InterVarsity Press, 1992. 335.
[134] Ibid. 67.

- The church (and individual believers) is therefore called to obediently join God on His mission—The *Missio Dei* is at the heart of the Great Commission: *"All authority in heaven and on earth has been given to me. [19] Therefore go and make disciples...."* (Mt. 28:18-20/Acts 8:1).
- Mission requires the mindset of believers to pivot from a centripetal—"church-centric" perspective, to a centrifugal view, that is, mission is centered in the identity, nature, and purposes of God—Mission is Christo-centric and therefore, it is culminated in the transforming power of the Gospel (e.g., Acts 8:4; 5-8).
- Missional entrepreneurs are always on mission (Mt. 28:20b).
- Mission is for the purpose of making the present kingdom of God tangible (reality) for defined people-groups in spiritual exile (e.g., Acts 8:5).
- Mission (plus liminal) is the catalytic "factor" in disciplemaking and cultural transformation (e.g., Acts 8:12, *et. al.* Lk. 10:1-24).
- The ultimate vision of mission is God's redemption of his creation—God is "making everything new!" (Rev. 21:5; 2 Cor. 5:17; Acts 8:25). And God invites us to join him in bringing into reality a new heaven and a new earth (Mt. 28:19/Rev. 21:1-7)!

How do we accept God's invitation and participate in the mission of God?
In his exposition of Psalm 147, Martin Luther spoke of the coupling of "the Priesthood of all Believers," and the "masks of God" to describe how God works through believers in their vocation and their everyday life (*et. al.*, Chapter 5, "Incarnational Mission").

INCARNATIONAL MISSION

"For us the Incarnation is an absolutely fundamental doctrine, not just as an irreducible part of the Christian confession, but also as a theological prism through which we view our entire missional task in the world."[135] Luther asserted, "God is the giver of all good gifts; but you must fall to, and take the bull by the horns, which means you must work to give God an occasion and a mask."[136] The "offering of spiritual sacrifices" focuses on Spirit-empowered priests (1 Peter 2:5) doing the works God has prepared in advance for us to do (Eph. 2:10) as "masks of God."

Luther's theological nuance, "masks of God," coupled with the Priesthood of all Believers, is what we refer to as incarnational mission, that is, missional practitioners perform as priests by creating spaces for God to work through them as his "mask," primarily their vocation; but one's vocation is not limited to where they work, it includes where "they do life" (any role God calls a believer to fill).[137]

Wherever a missionally driven disciple does life, incarnational mission is at the center of their activities. Incarnational mission calls the missionally driven disciple to incarnate the Word and Spirit of the Lord. Micah 6:8 introduces a concise (three-fold) biblical theology of incarnational mission:

---

[135] Michael Frost & Alan Hirsch. *The Shaping of Things To Come.* Peabody, MA.: Hendrickson Publishers, 2003. 35.

[136] Luther on God's 'Masks,' Martin Luther's exposition of Psalm 147. Posted August 29, 2012, The Rev 2011 in Church History, Providence, Reformed Piety & Christian Nurture. https://christcovenantopc.wordpress.com/2012/08/29/luther-on-gods-masks/. Downloaded: 12/12/2019

[137] See the outstanding book: Samuel Wells. *Incarnational Mission, Being With the World.* Grand Rapids, MI.: William B. Eerdmans Publishing Company, 2018.

MICAH 6:8c—"ACT JUSTLY"

"To act justly ... "

Missional entrepreneurs engaging in incarnational mission are *"to act justly,"* or "do justice;" "act" or "do" are verbs. We are required to obediently engage justice. The Hebrew term translated "act justly" (*mispat*) finds "its source in God himself and therefore carrying with it his demand."[138]

In the Old Testament, this term (*mispat*) is connected to widows, orphans, the poor, the needy, the oppressed, the stranger, the prisoner, and the fatherless (Isa. 1:17; Isa. 61:1-2, cf. Lk. 4:18-19; Isa. 58:6-7).[139] To "act justly" connects the believer to people living on the extreme margins of culture (that is, people in the greatest need)—*Our relationship with God directly relates to how we care for these people.*

"In the study of the history of missions," Alan Hirsch observes, "one can even be formulaic about asserting that *all great missionary movements begin at the fringes of the church,* among the poor and the marginalized, and seldom, if ever, at the center."[140] Mission focused on the extreme margins of culture is consistently liminal and therefore, catalytic in the life of "masked priests," i.e., missional practitioners on incarnational mission. And through obedience to the modeling of her Lord *"... when the church engages at the fringes, it almost always brings life to the center."*[141]

The disciples' obedience (cf. Acts 8:1-25) leads them into a liminal situation in which they are confronted by spiritual strongholds—malignant

---

[138] Harris, Archer, Jr., and Waltke, *Theological Wordbook of the Old Testament,* Vol. II (Chicago, IL.: Moody Press, 1980), 948-49.

[139] Brown, Driver, and Briggs, *Hebrew and English Lexicon,* (490), 48; (3490), 450, (1800), 195, (34), 2, (7533), 954, (1616), 158, (615/16), 64, (3490), 450.

[140] Alan Hirsch, *The Forgotten Ways,* 30.

[141] Ibid. 30.

spirits, and racial prejudice—their own, and the Samaritans'—Jesus' disciples have no idea how the Lord's divinely ordered mission is going to turn out, but they are, never-the-less, obedient (Acts 8:6-11).

MICAH 6:8c—"LOVE MERCY"

"... and to love mercy..."

"Christ in us" compels us to "love mercy." The Hebrew term (*hesed*) is related to our understanding of "compassion." The Latin understanding is more precise however: we are to *"co-suffer, to come alongside of"* the hurting, the weak, the vulnerable and the poor.

God's love means many things in Scripture. But God's "delivering love" is consistent throughout the Bible—*God's love is consistently demonstrated in Scripture as a delivering action*. The Parable of the Good Samaritan is a vivid example of God's delivering love. The parable is Jesus' answer to the lawyer's question, "Who is my neighbor?" The point of the parable is to teach us *how* and *whom* we should love.[142]

A Samaritan man sees a Jewish man, who after having been attacked by robbers, was stripped of his clothing, beaten and left half dead on the side of the road (Lk. 10:30). The Samaritan is described as having pity on this man. The Greek term translated "pity" or "compassion" refers to a "gut-feeling."[143] The Samaritan's response is intense, it is a strong emotional response followed by a delivering act of love—*Drawn by compassion, the Samaritan enters the situation of the helpless, wounded Jewish man*. By contrast, the priest and the Levite are described in strong terms as "moving

---

[142] John Dominic Crossan. *In Parables*. New York: Harper & Row, 1973, 57. Quoted in: Glen H. Stassen & David P. Gushee. *Kingdom Ethics*, 334.
[143] Glenn Stassen & David Gushee, *Kingdom Ethics*, 335.

away." Jesus tells this story in a way that emphasizes that compassion moves toward need and identifies with the need, to include our enemies.[144]

To love mercy, you must be where the pain is, because God is hidden in the pain. By throwing yourself into a place of pain, you discover the joy of Jesus. All ministry in the history of the church is built on a vision of *holistic redemption,* that is, ministry is committed to the common good of the culture by its unashamed, single-minded commitment to the Cross, and the dynamic power of the Holy Spirit's presence in the lives of believers (Acts 8:12).

Mission (ministry) is for helping people discover that in the middle of pain there is hope and blessing. In our world, there is an enormous distinction between good and bad, sorrow and joy, but in God's eyes, they are never separated: where there is pain, there is healing; where there is mourning, there is dancing; and where there is poverty, there is the riches of the kingdom (Acts 8:14-17).

MICAH 6:8d—WALK HUMBLY

"… and to walk humbly with your God"

And God requires us to: *"walk humbly."* The Hebrew term translated "walk humbly" literally means, "creating space."[145] We are to "create space" or environments for the kingdom of God to be made tangible in the lives of those living in exile, people without Christ, without life and without hope (Acts 8:25).

We are to see the staggering needs in our world and acknowledge that God is before all other things in our lives: ourselves, our family, our friends,

---

[144] Ibid.
[145] Brown, Driver, and Briggs, *Hebrew, and English Lexicon*, 857a, 6800 (Hiph. *Inf.abs.*)

our life's goals and aspirations, our personal security and comfort, *everything*. We are called to take the place of others and see the physical and spiritual needs in our community and the world and ask ourselves: *"What can I do for the person I see across the street, across my office space, on my work site, on the other side of my city, across the world?"*[146]

The missional congregation is to join God by identifying a specific group in exile—e.g., those enslaved in sex-trafficking, addicts, the homeless, those in multi-housing projects, prisoners, at-risk youth, etc., and create environments, e.g., low-income housing, trailer parks, coffee houses, training centers, etc.[147] Incarnational mission requires our obedience by way of making ourselves available for God, as mediators (priests) for His works to flow through us to those alienated from God (cf. Genesis 12:3b).

As they stand in the space between God and the Samaritans, the disciples took their place alongside of the Samaritans, and in obedience to Christ, they loved their enemies and proclaimed the Gospel to them with an acute awareness of the cultural expectations of the Samaritans—*They exchanged their racial prejudice for identification with the Samaritans in their exile* (Acts 8:1-25).

Following a missional reading of scripture, and a thorough parsing of principles and practices that flow from the *Missio Dei*, we are ready to formulate a missional theology.

---

[146] My thoughts are inspired by Paul Hurkman, *Venture Expeditions,* contained in a sermon delivered at Cedar Valley Church, Bloomington, MN., January 13, 2013.

[147] Consistent with the nature of the Incarnation is the Spirit's drawing of Jesus to those in the greatest need—the indigent, the disenfranchised and outcasts. Jesus' missional sights are consistently set on a *specific* group or individual (cf. Lk. 4:18-19; Mt. 11:4-6). And through God's delivering love, Jesus takes the place of those in spiritual, social, economic exile—*Consistently, Jesus' missional patterns primarily means that he works from the margins to the center, rather than the reverse.*

A MISSIONAL THEOLOGY

> *Every believer is to involve themselves "... in the eternal purposes of God in the world to redeem it to Himself, to sum up all things to Himself in Christ Jesus"*[148]

The *Missio Dei* —The Mission of God— is the nucleus of a missional theology. And therefore, the *Missio Dei* is the primary *cause* of missional congregations.

Missional texts saturate both the Old Testament and the New Testament—The *"... whole Bible is itself a 'missional' phenomenon."*[149] A missional reading of the biblical text (e.g., Acts 8:1-25) enables the believer to see that the Scripture itself is the result of and witness to the *Missio Dei*—A missional theology is formulated around the *Missio Dei* and the layers of missional praxis that flow from God's invitation to join Him on mission.

The eternal Trinity is the Author of mission: The Father *sent* the Son; the Father and the Son *sent* the Spirit, and the Spirit sends missional congregations—*God is a sending (Latin, missio) God. Believers are sent by God to join Him on His mission (the Missio Dei)—Mission was not made for the church; the church was made for mission.*

And therefore, any space-time missional enterprise flows from the prior reality of God's eternal mission (*Missio Dei*). Consequently, the Lord does not send his disciples ahead of himself, he is always waiting for us to come, and when we show up, he empowers us to join him, and witness the flow of his mission through us—*In their priestly role, missional practitioners stand in the space between people in exile and God; and as masks of God, practitioners*

---

[148] Allan Hirsch. "What is Missional Discipleship?" https://www.youtube.com/watch?v=WhEwxSQ5tqA. Downloaded: 02/28/2019.

[149] Christopher Wright. *The Mission of God*. 22.

engage in incarnational mission: God works through missional practitioners to make known the present reality of the kingdom of God.

The *Missio Dei* engages all of life, to include all legitimate vocations—all work, e.g., waiter, physician, construction, truck driver, logger, lawyer, grocery clerk, custodian, teacher, airman, sailor, soldier, marine, police officer, etc. These vocations are sacred callings, no less than a pastor, bishop, or missionary. *And therefore, all missional practitioners are always on mission with God, restoring the environment, renewing cultures, and rescuing people by offering healing and hope.*

Ultimately, a missional theology informs the redemptive purposes of God, climatically concluding in the ultimate achievement of "The Great Commission"—Revelation 7:9-10:

> *[9] After this I looked, and there before me was a great multitude that no one could count, from every nation, tribe, people and language, standing before the throne and before the Lamb.*
>
> *They were wearing white robes and were holding palm branches in their hands. [10] And they cried out in a loud voice:*
>
> *"Salvation belongs to our God,*
> *who sits on the throne,*
> *and to the Lamb."*

MISSIONAL THEOLOGY: THE MISSIO DEI AND ITS MISSIONAL ORBIT

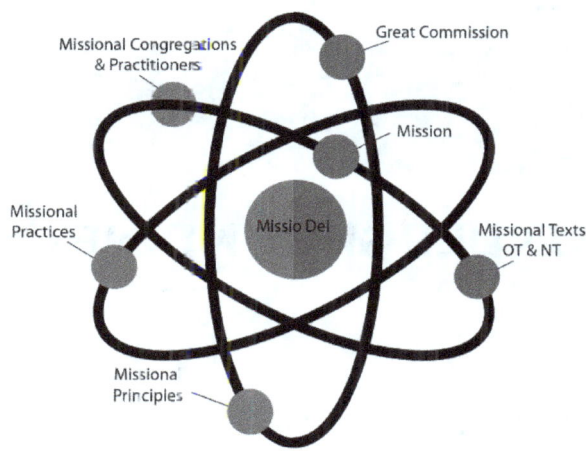

[150]

Chapters 8-16 are interviews conducted with pastors of missional congregations, directors of Christian organizations and managers of third places. Please critically observe how these select missional congregations, organizations, and third places "live missionally beyond Sunday!"

More specifically, observe how they engage and transform the cultural rhythms of their host communities by uniquely modeling a missional theology in imaginative, creative, and diverse ways through incarnational mission. And finally, please observe that a coherent missional theology is not prescriptive but rather, as viewed through the lens of Biblical Revelation, it is contextual, and therefore, it is nuanced in ways that serve the purposes of the *Missio Dei* in a particular location.

---

[150] Neurons and Electrons Images: https://www.shutterstock.com/search/neutrons+and+electrons

CHAPTER 8

THE UNDERGROUND NETWORK

TAMPA BAY, FLORIDA

"*Become the church, and that starts with mission*" —Brian Sanders

The Underground incarnates a vision of "*MORE!*"[151] Tomy Wilkerson is Tampa Director of the Underground Network. I opened my interview with Tomy by asking him, "Where did the founders of 'The Underground' begin in their search 'for more'?" Tomy reflected on Brian Sanders' ministry in 1995 with Intervarsity Christian Fellowship on the campus of the University of South Florida.

Brian's work with Christian students not only involved reaching the campus of the University of South Florida, but also serving the poor in the city of Tampa. Brian comments, "The first program our group started was a tutoring project, followed by a summer-long poverty 'immersion project' meant to help university students encounter God in the beauty and pain

---

[151] See the story of the Underground: https://vimeo.com/256315051

of an American inner city."[152] Brian further reflected on the students' work among the poor as a means of discipling them: "To my mind, the students were the mission, the inner city was the classroom, and the poor were the professors."[153]

Missional engagement to the poor meant identifying with them by sleeping outside on the streets; students began to develop a missionary identity. "They understood mission, witness, care for the poor, and radical community only through the lens of our work," observes Brian.[154] And further, notes Brian, "There was little dissonance between the lives they were trying to lead and the pages of Scripture."[155]

As the students graduated and began to assimilate into society, many of them experienced disillusionment in the local church; a radical disconnect existed between what they experienced on campus and among the poor in Tampa, and what they were experiencing in the traditional church—helping park cars, raising money for more comfortable and decorative seats in the sanctuary and signing up to serve the church in various, prescribed ways. They could not reconcile missional patterns in Scripture with the structures, centralization, and attractional commitments of the traditional church.

Soon, many among the disillusioned and frustrated began to come together and pursue God for more; they were unclear about what "more" was, but they resolved to begin a journey together by asking a simple, foundational question: "If you strip everything away that is not essential to being a church, what are you left with?" One evening in 2002 in the safety of the Sanders' living room, about fifty disaffected campus ministry

---

[152] Brian Sanders. *Underground Church*. 30.
[153] Ibid.
[154] Ibid., 31.
[155] Ibid.

graduates concluded that they were left with, worship, community, and mission—"What makes a group of people a church is that they worship together, are committed to each other, and undertake mission together."[156]

Several dozen of the disenchanted alumni lived near one another. And they began meeting in five house churches and engaging in mission work in Tampa. Their vision "was to pursue that *more,* and to do it together."[157]

THE PHILIPPINES—IDENTITY WITH THE POOR

> *"We left because we were alive with the hope of the kingdom of God at work in and through the people of God"*—Brian Sanders.

In the Fall of 2006, following a series of events and prophetic exhortations,[158] nine adults and ten children set out on a journey to Manila, the capital of the Philippines. Brian Sanders found a row of small dwellings in the slums of Quezon City, a large city in the greater metropolitan area of Manila.[159] The missionaries gave themselves up to God in prayer and hope that He would work through the poor in the developing world to help them understand how to conform the contemporary church to "the vision of Jesus in the New Testament."[160]

Three significant things became seeds of the emerging "more": (1) Wherever you see worship, community, and mission, you see the formation of ecclesiology, you see the church; (2) A dual operating system; on one side, is the decentralized church—networks of small, scattered enterprises, and on the other side is the centralized nonprofit committed to serving the small, vulnerable expressions of the church. And (3) a unique ecosystem

---

[156] Ibid., 34.
[157] Ibid., 38-39.
[158] 1 Cor. 14:2-3 KJV.
[159] Brian Sanders. *Underground Church*. 41.
[160] Ibid.

that operates underneath the [Biblical] assumption that every believer is called and sent by Jesus.

This invisible, underground ecosystem, unique to the emergent dream (the "More") and embodied in the lives of the fifty ecclesia refugees is the source of a name intended to honor the persecuted, underground church in the world.[161] "The Underground" became official in 2007 after the missionary team returned from the Philippines.

"Our dream," writes Sanders, "was of a church encountering Jesus on the margins, and of a world whirling from being loved so fiercely by a church on fire for God."[162] The Underground's dream is grounded in The Lausanne Covenant (1974) and the reaffirmations of the Manila Manifesto (1989). The coupling of these documents with the "Philippines' dream" is uniquely expressed in The Underground Manifesto.[163]

20% SERVING 80%—THE TRADITIONAL MODEL OF THE CHURCH

Tomy observes that the traditional model of the church features the pastor and his/her pastoral staff as "the best of us." They exclusively (contrary to congregational members) possess specialized training, knowledge, and experience and therefore, the church leadership is the epitome of what we all need to be.

A mission's pastor is hired to apply his or her expertise to mission commitments of the church, both domestic and foreign, the youth pastor creates a following among teenage believers, and the music pastor assembles

---

[161] Ibid. 49
[162] Ibid. 48
[163] Re: The Manifesto and Values of the Underground, see: Tampa Underground Network. https://www.tampaunderground.com/our-story-index#manifesto-intro. Who We Are/Values. Downloaded: 12/17/2021.

worship teams and leads the church in how they should worship the Lord. The lead pastor distributes the work of the ministry among his or her pastoral staff.

The pastoral staff recruits volunteers from the congregation to coordinate "ministry" roles for church members such as greeters, parking attendents, nursery, children church workers, Women's and Men's Ministry, and sound techs.

Congregational members are primarily spectators and recipients ("consumers") of the church leadership's spiritual/religious "goods"—As spectators, congregational members support the leadership's vision through prayer, their Sunday morning attendance, and by volunteering for, and funding the centralized spiritual enterprises of the church. The traditional church model flows downward for professional clergy and upwards for congregational members:

[164].

---

[164] The Underground Network: https://www.undergroundnetwork.org/who-we-are-index/#new-model. Downloaded: 12/08/21.

Brian Sanders writes, "Confronted with the hard reality of the prevailing model of church, I could see the church was being used to serve the least productive 80 percent."[165] Sanders provides further clarity, "This means that the most potent and apostolic people are either rejected or repurposed for some internal project, instead of being utilized for outward mission."[166] Sanders' resolve is reforming, *"What if we built an organization that was not just fueled by the 20 percent, but one that actually existed for and was run by them?"*[167]

MISSIONAL THEOLOGY—INVERTING THE TRADITIONAL WESTERN MODEL

I asked Tomy, *"How is the priesthood of all believers manifest in The Underground Network?"* Tomy's answer adroitly couples the prayer and hope of the Philippine missionaries with the "vision of Jesus in the New Testament." The formulation of a missional theology, in the thought and mission of The Underground, is threefold: (1) Ecclesiology—Wherever you see worship, community and mission, the ecclesiology of The Underground is being fleshed out. (2) A dual operating system—The ecclesiology of The Underground is one side of the operating system; the other side is a non-profit mission-agency. And (3) The autonomy of "microchurches"—the uniqueness of The Underground is its cultivation of a decentralized ecosystem that operates under the assumption that every believer is called and sent by Jesus.

Brian Sanders, The Underground's founder, further develops the essence of a missional theology. *"Church is made up of its people, who are all apostles (missionaries); its equippers, who are servants; and its infrastructure, which is*

---

[165] Brian Sanders. *Underground Church*. 55.
[166] Ibid.
[167] Ibid.

centrifugal (moves outward). Equippers need, therefore, to help, empower, and pledge to meet the needs of those who meet the needs of others."[168] A model of the Underground's missional ecclesiology is an inversion (plus microchurches) of the traditional church model:

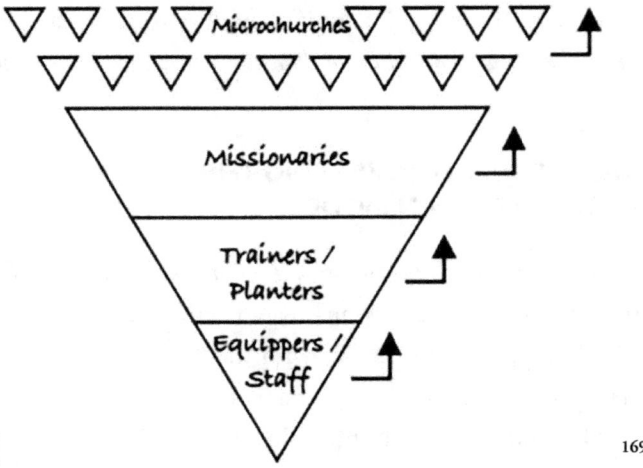

[169]

Tomy emphasizes that, "We don't try to get anybody to sign up for the church's programs" but to the contrary, the primary undertaking of the nonprofit mission agency is to serve microchurches by proactively discovering what is in the hearts of missional entrepreneurs: "What has the Lord called you to do?" "What is your assignment?" And the principal undertaking of leadership is to continually ask, "What do the microchurches need to be the church God called them to be?" "We"—the nonprofit mission agency—inspires, equips, trains, networks, prays for, supports, and celebrates every individual called by Jesus to do what He has placed in their

---

[168] Ibid. 55-56.
[169] The Underground: https://www.undergroundnetwork.org/who-we-are-index/#new-model. Downloaded: 12/08/21.

heart[170]—*In a word, the ecclesial model of the Underground empowers the (micro) church to be the church!*

MICROCHURCHES—THE CHURCH DOES NOT SEND, IT IS SENT

> *"In only a decade, the Underground Network has become an ecclesial structure that reaches the lost and poor in Tampa Bay by planting what they call microchurches—small, missional communities that all usher in God's kingdom in a unique way"*—Alan Hirsch.[171]

Tomy reinforces his emphasis above by stressing that in The Underground, "the staff is not the heroes of the story, but rather the microchurches are the heroes." The nonprofit mission-agency exists to serve the missional enterprise of microchurches—Microchurches listen to Jesus, and the nonprofit serves in any way necessary to enable microchurches to be obedient to the Lord. The outcome of the inversion of the traditional church model to a missional incarnational model is the "leadership," that is, equippers and staff, reaching upward to serve missional entrepreneurs in whatever way Jesus calls them to their priestly work.

As microchurches join Jesus on His mission, they manifest the priesthood of all believers in diverse ways, by meeting diverse needs throughout the city—The *Missio Dei* is at the core of the decentralized ecosystem of the Underground.

"Over the course of time," observes Tomy, "we've identified two different kinds of microchurches: mission-specific and distributive. Microchurches that are mission-specific are joined together by aiming to reach a particular

---

[170] See the Underground Website: https://www.tampaunderground.com/. The Resources tab features an impressive listing of the Underground's training opportunities: https://www.tampaunderground.com/resources/#mission-resources.

[171] Allan Hirsch. Foreword, *Underground Church*.

demographic—e.g., "Bible at the Bar," for bikers who are finding Jesus in the bar, "Fresh-Start," for those lost, incarcerated, and in transition, "Heart-Dance Foundation," for those fighting human trafficking, "Mama Africana," for Black girls, "PB & J," for serving the poor of Tampa, "Sisters Made of Clay," for providing transitional housing for women, "Solo Moms," for single moms, "Support 4 Caregivers," for caregivers of children with disabilities, "Timothy Initiative," for men in recovery, "Urban Youth Justice," for incarcerated youth, "Underground Clinic," for those in need of healthcare, "Well-Spring Community Farm," for health food and life, etc.[172] (In Tampa, 75 microchurches serve the diverse needs of a diverse population throughout the city).

Distributive microchurches, on the other hand, have a gathering space that then acts as an incubator for diverse kinds of mission. Some people will be called to reach their workplace, others their neighborhood, some, their "third places"[173]

The Nonprofit Mission Agency provides the microchurches with training, finance, coaching, facilities, and media towards their success. And although the Mission Agency does not tell the microchurches how to do disciplemaking, they offer an impressive inventory of resources to teach, train, and equip the microchurches' leadership.[174]

The church does not send, it is sent and for The Underground, "… microchurches can and should be as diverse as the people who start them."[175]

---

[172] Tampa Underground Network. https://www.tampaunderground.com/microchurches. Downloaded: 12/17/2021.

[173] "Third Places" are among the ways missional congregations create environments for God to move in the lives of those in diverse socio-cultural contexts. Please see Chapter 15, "Third Places."

[174] Re: The Underground Network. Resources. https://www.tampaunderground.com/resources. Downloaded: 12/18/2021.

[175] Brian Sanders. *Microchurches, (a smaller way)*. Underground Media, 2019. 63.

Therefore, the Nonprofit Mission Agency is built for the community on mission—"Once people within our influence understand their calling, we connect them to collaborative communities of people who share the same calling. None of us is sent alone. Finding those who share our calling is a real need."[176]

There are currently fifteen movements in the Underground Network. Alongside Tampa Underground, the expanding Underground Network includes Common Thread, Alabama, Narrative Church, Arkansas, Lantern Network, Illinois, Wildfire, Texas, Ignite, Dublin, Ireland, Yangon, Myanmar, Manila Underground, Philippines, HOPE, Dominican Republic, Paris, France, Kansas City Underground, Catalyst Network, Portland, Zoe, Toronto, Be the Church Network, Atlanta, Center Network, and The Canvas Network, St. Louis.[177]

---

[176] Brian Sanders. *Underground Church*. 58.
[177] See Tampa Underground Network, https://www.tampaunderground.com/our-story-index/#story-welcome, "Who We Are," Global Movements, https://www.undergroundnetwork.org/.

CHAPTER 9

FATHER'S HOUSE

PORTLAND, OR

"IN PORTLAND *as it is* IN HEAVEN"

When Steve Trujillo was 9-years old, his family left Cuba and flew to Spain. From Spain, his family went to New York City. From New York, the Trujillo family began to travel throughout the United States visiting old friends and family. Eventually, the Trujillo's settled in Portland, Oregon due to a relationship with a pastor there whose church sponsored the Trujillo family and helped them immigrate from Spain to the U.S. and then move to Portland.

Steve informed me that as he deboarded the plane at PDX and gazed towards Portland, the Lord clearly spoke to him (a ten-year old boy at the time) and said, "You are at the place of your destiny." Pastor Steve is motivated everyday by that promise as he begins each morning caring for his church and making disciples, who themselves, make disciples in the city they love, Portland, Oregon.

Father's House was founded by Steve and his wife, Deborah, over 20 years ago. Father's House originally occupied the space of a former Korean church in downtown Portland but after 5 years they moved to a building at the center of Portland State University's campus. (The Father's House's connection to Portland State University is typical of their unique missional approach. I will develop this story in the context of Father's House's fuller story below).

The mission of Father's House is: "At Father's House, we seek to live as family on mission to our world." Pastor Steve's sense of his church's purpose informs him of how he should measure his church's success: Father's House should not be measured by how many adherents come together to worship on Sunday morning but rather, if Father's House were no longer in the center of Portland, would Portland cry?

I asked Pastor Trujillo, how do you choose certain people-groups to engage in mission?

Pastor Steve is emphatic about the indispensable role of prayer regarding God's choice for those Father's House missional teams need to connect with. Prayer has led Pastor Trujillo to wisely inquire about needs in Portland by asking city leaders what they believe are the greatest needs in the city.

This approach is rarely taken by pastors, instead, pastors generally assume they know what the needs of the city are, and they therefore ignore city leaders as they set out to address needs. (Interestingly, pastors in downtown Portland consistently assume that they need a meal program and consequently, if a homeless person is hungry enough, he or she can eat seven meals a day in the central city).

Pastor Trujillo described an occasion when the Portland City Commissioner was addressing a room full of people, among them were several pastors from the Portland metropolitan area. The Commissioner directly addressed the pastors informing them that they too often do what they think the city wants, but they never talk to anyone who works for the city; they never ask him or any of the city officials. The Commissioner stated, "You need to be more like Steve Trujillo, who knows what it is to be at the table."

Steve asserts, "Every city has a 'table' that local government listens to." And because Steve "knows what it is to be at the table," Steve has gained favor with many city leaders and consequently, he has been given opportunities to influence public policy. For example, he served for 6 years as the president of the Downtown Neighborhood Association. Steve is presently the president of the Neighborhood Association. (And he is also involved with public safety).

Consequently, Pastor Trujillo knows the hearts of those who most influence public policy in Portland. And from his place "at the table," Steve speaks directly to the hearts of Portland leadership—Steve's place at "the table" has not only given him favor with Portland leaders, but also city influencers at a variety of socio-political levels. Steve has gained the unique opportunity to "become all things to all people so that by all possible means [he] might save some" (1 Cor. 9:22).

Speaking of God giving Steve favor among those who hold positions of influence, it may have occurred to you that Portland State University is a secular university, and therefore, how is a church able to have offices, and do worship services in the center of PSU's property? From where Steve "sits at the table," he connected with a gracious man who is the overseer of all of Portland State University's properties. God gave Steve favor with this influential man, and he offered Steve and his church space in a building located in the center of the campus. Father's House offices ended up in the university's Philosophy Department!

As a centerpiece of Father's House's commitment to mission, Pastor Trujillo leads groups on regular "prayer-walks" throughout the neighborhood surrounding Father's House. On one occasion, Pastor Trujillo sent one of his mission's teams to pray for a particular business near their church. The owner of the business saw the group praying, and she went out to the edge of her property to meet them. The business owner asked the team leader if he and his group were praying for her business. The team's leader said, yes and the lady was deeply moved, and she enthusiastically expressed her gratitude to them.

Soon after the COVID virus began to alter much of American life, Steve and the church had to vacate the University because they shut it down. God provided a temporary warehouse space for the church. But soon Steve was informed that the landlord did not want the church there and they had eight days to relocate. Steve had no place to go, but he reminded the church how God had provided the warehouse after PSU shut down, and he assured the church that God will provide again.

Shortly after that last service in the warehouse, Pastor Steve was contacted by a woman who had been on the prayer assignment to the nearby business. She told him, "Come back I got the keys to a building for us." Steve met the woman from the team and a woman, who owned the business the team had prayed for. The woman also owned a building that had been a famous restaurant in Portland. Many who worked in that restaurant where highly involved in witchcraft.

Steve was informed by a church plant member, who had applied to work there years earlier that some employees would perform witchcraft related rituals in the basement. This restaurant space became the new location for Father's House!

Among the missional foci of Father's House is "Tomorrow's Hope," a human trafficking intervention ministry which was a direct result of the prayers at the Downtown House of Prayer, a space where about thirty-five churches in Portland pray together, daily, for the city. The churches bathe

Portland in prayer, often-times as many as 96 hours a week, focusing on needs; principal among them is human trafficking. Eventually twelve churches in Portland became involved in the Transformation Network which became the collaborative arm to facilitate the ministry of Tomorrow's Hope. Each of the twelve churches have a critical role in addressing human trafficking in the Portland Metro area.

Primary "targets" of human traffickers' range in age from 11-17 years old (though older young adults and adults are also trafficked). Father's House has been involved with finding kids in Portland who are enslaved by traffickers and rescuing them. They [the victims] are then placed in safe places that work towards the victim's recovery and safe return to either family or a guardian.[178]

In 2011, the Transformation Network birthed Tomorrow's Hope which was then led by Father's House members to reach children and adults trapped in the evil snares of human trafficking. Portland was the number one city in the nation for human trafficking. Portland is now ranked number twenty-one (21).[179] Pastor Trujillo acknowledges that strategic on the ground prayer has been the greatest force behind Portland's decent among U.S. cities' human trafficking rankings.

I asked Pastor Trujillo how he sees the role of the Missional Congregation in relation to Western Civilization's present socio-cultural and political divide. Instead of a broad, general response, Steve focused on Father's

---

[178] Pastor Trujillo shared with me that Father's House is in desperate need of housing for human trafficking victims.

[179] National Human Trafficking Hotline, Ranking of the Most Populus US Cities, 12/7/2007 – 12/31/2016. https://humantraffickinghotline.org/sites/default/files/100%20Most%20Populous%20Cities%20Report.pdf. Downloaded: 02/12/2021. (I have diligently searched for 2020 stats; perhaps I am unable to find newer stats because reportedly, agencies find that relative cases are reported, and statistics are difficult to provide.

House's sense of mission and purpose in Portland. Mission flows from God, and therefore, Pastor Trujillo seeks to join Jesus Christ wherever He is on mission and do the works God prepared in advance for himself, and his missional team members to do.

As I write (09/2021) Portland has been at the center of national news reporting, particularly regarding the siege of the city for more than one-hundred and fifty consecutive days by protesters. Violent protests have been primarily aimed at the Justice Center which contains Police headquarters and the county jail, and the federal courthouse. Also attacked was the Portland Police Bureau's North and East Precincts, the Portland Police Association Building, the Multnomah County Building in SE Portland, and ICE offices in SW Portland, although many businesses have also been torched.

Father's House missional teams have been making Christ known to both police and protesters, particularly at the Federal and Justice Buildings in downtown Portland. Missional teams from Father's House let the police know that they are praying for them, their safety and ability to enforce the law. (Because of his place at "the table," PPB welcomes Pastor Steve and his missional prayer teams). And Father's House missionaries have also told the police that they are praying among the protesters/rioters and seeking to engage them with the Gospel.

During the riots, protesters, one at a time, or two or three together have been drawn to Father's House missional team members and they have asked them about Jesus Christ and the Gospel they are sharing. There, amid the mayhem, fires and arrests, protesters have been giving their lives to Christ!

Prayer is effective at Father's House because of bold, "faith-risking" missions—The more liminal, the deeper, wider, and higher is the experience of communitas among those who believe in prayer at Father's House!

Additionally, Father's House is ever-expanding its influence through the church's School of City Transformation. The school focuses its courses on "Seven Keys of Transformation."

Recently (2020-21), the School of City Transformation graduated fifty students. In 2020,

COVID forced the School of Transformation to pivot from in-person classes to online. Soon, thirty to forty new students will be studying city transformation online.

Shortly after arriving at the University, the Lord began speaking to Steve's heart about serving the campus and soon, He highlighted married students with children at PSU. Steve began walking through the Portland State campus and talking with the Lord about how Father's House could reach young families at PSU. At the conclusion of his walk, and prayer, Steve went to his mailbox to check his mail. A letter to a different recipient had been misplaced in Steve's mailbox. Printed on the outside of the envelope was, "Thank you for your interest and commitment to students with children at Portland State University"!

I started to ask Steve a foolish question, but I stopped short of it, although I shared it with him, "Do you ever do anything in a conventional way?" What a foolish notion! If a man or woman is walking with the Lord, and doing His will, nothing is ever "conventional"! Pastor Steve agreed with me!

I asked Pastor Trujillo about Father's House's commitment to the Great Commission. God's mission for Father's House includes the church's commitment to foreign students at Portland State University. Foreign students come from all over the world to study at PSU, and they leave to return to their nations as people of influence. Father's House seeks to disciple foreign students who then return home as disciples who make disciples. This is an extremely critical role Father's House embraces towards the achievement of the Great Commission.

Because of COVID, Father's House began gathering for Wednesday evening worship and community services outside to the street where they would just take over a block in their Portland neighborhood. Pastor Trujillo rejoiced with me as he shared how people, walking by stopped, and came up to him, or other worshippers, and asked how they could receive Christ into their lives! While celebrating Jesus in Portland's Pioneer Square, three Middle Eastern men drove up and parked. They observed the Father's House worshippers for a short while before getting out of their car and approaching an evangelism team member and asking him how they could know Jesus Christ as their Savior!

Steve shared how people throughout the city have been searching for greater meaning because of the disillusionment created by night-after-night of riots and the burning of their city and the political opposition to their safety and welfare, especially when it comes to the defunding of the Portland P.D.—There is a great move of God in Portland, beginning on the margins, among the most vulnerable, and it's beginning to the impact the center!

"You don't get what you don't celebrate," remarked Pastor Trujillo. On Sunday morning, various outreach team members come up in front of the church to share great testimonies, experiences, and stories from going to the streets during the week. This generates faith and vision for others to go out and do the same. So, Father's House clearly defines that "missional is the exchanging of darkness for light!"

Among Sunday morning testimonies, one that has "stood out" for Steve was shared by a young woman who began by saying, "The place where Satan defeated me, is where I want to defeat him!" This young woman suffered a psychotic breakdown requiring her to be institutionalized—She was empty, broken and defeated. During her long, painful recovery, she discovered strength in Christ. Once she was restored by Jesus Christ, she began her studies to earn the necessary degree to return to the hospital where she was institutionalized. She now works at that institution, caring for and counseling people with borderline personality disorders.

Would Portland Oregon "cry" if Father's House were no longer in the center of the city? I confess that I would cry—Portland is my hometown, and after interviewing Pastor Steve Trujillo, I am convinced that God has not given up on the "Rose City."

CHAPTER 10

JACOB'S WELL

KANSAS CITY, MO.

> *"We Are a Community of People*
> *FOLLOWING JESUS*
> *And Learning to Live in His Ways"*[180]

Before my interview with Pastor Keel, I viewed a message Tim delivered from Ephesians 3:14-21. Tim shared an illustration involving the extensive root patterns of an old tree in the Keel's backyard, a part of which grew beneath the patio, causing the bricks to breakup. Tim's wife, Mimi, removed the broken bricks and, consequently, the patio, exposing the tree's root-network. In a different context, Andy Crouch remarked on how Jacob's Well is rooted in its own particular neighborhood in a way that would be very difficult to replicate elsewhere (Crouch commented that "It made me want to move to Kansas City. Really").

---

[180] https://www.jacobswellchurch.org/. 06/07/2021.

I asked Tim, "How is Andy Crouch's description of how Jacob's Well is uniquely "rooted" in Kansas City connected to the root patterns of the tree in your backyard and, the missional patterns you employ to transform your cultural context?"

Tim responded by first observing the legacy of the church created by American consumerism: We measure the success of a church by the size of its budget, its offerings and congregational size. Consumerism reduces "truth" to whatever works and applies a model wherein spiritual wisdom is exchanged for marketing principles—Christian spirituality is then reduced to the marketing of religious goods.

But Jacob's Well's spirituality cannot be reduced to a series of principles; you cannot understand Jacob's Well without its worship leader, Mike Crawford—Ministry flows organically out of identity and like the tree in the Keel's backyard, it takes a long time to take root. In fact, Tim described how after 5 ½ years into the life of Jacob's Well, it looked a lot more like what he didn't want it to be before it began to look like what he wanted it to be. Tim discovered that his church plant was much less about the philosophy behind it, and much more about deeply rooted relationships—intimate connections, throughout Kansas City.

"The whole point of Jacob's Well is to build a church for the church"—[4] *"Abide in Me, and I in you. As the branch cannot bear fruit of itself, unless it abides in the vine, neither can you, unless you abide in Me"* (Jn 15:4, NKJV). "Abide," as used in John 15:4, is an imperative stressing the only way to continue "clean" (pruned) and bear fruit is to maintain a dynamic, spiritual connection to Jesus Christ, the Vine[181]—"It is essential

---

[181] BAGD, 504. A.T. Robertson. *Word Pictures in the New Testament.* John 15:4. Grand Rapids, MI.: Baker Book House. 1932. 258.

for the disciples, if they are to fulfill the task which is laid upon them that they should abide in fellowship with Jesus, who gives them their vitality."[182]

Ministry is a byproduct of abiding; abiding is for communities.[183] To press this point, Pastor Keel posed the question: *"What does it look like to build a community of people that allows them to abide and out of that become intimately connected to the vine?"*

Tim reflected on a timeless insight authored by Lesslie Newbigin, "How can this strange story of God made flesh, of a crucified Savior, of resurrection and new creation become credible for those whose entire mental training has conditioned them to believe that the real world is the world which can be satisfactorily explained and managed without the hypothesis of God? I know of only one clue to the answering of that question, only one real hermeneutic of the gospel: a congregation which believes it."[184]

Dallas Willard's observation punctuates Newbigin's "hermeneutic of the gospel," "How to combine faith with obedience is surely the essential task of the church as it enters the twenty-first century.[185] Indeed, this "essential task," makes credible the church's professed belief in "this strange story of God made flesh, of a crucified Savior, of resurrection and new creation."

Jacob's Well's unique identity organically flows through an intricate, intentional "root system" formed over a period of several years—Little wonder exists why it is difficult to replicate and attempts to do so would not be wise. But "root systems" designed to fit the *unique identity* of other

---

[182] Joh. W. Behm. G. Kittel, Editor. *Theological Dictionary of the New Testament.* Vol. III, 757.

[183] Jacob's Well is a model of "communitas." See Allan Hirsch. *The Forgotten Ways.* "*Communitas,* not community" (Chapter 8), 217-241.

[184] Lesslie Newbigin. *Missionary Theologian,* A Reader. Extract 1, "Evangelism and the City," (1987). Compiled by: Paul Westin. Grand Rapids, MI. Wm. B. Eerdmans, 2006. 144.

[185] Dallas Willard. *Divine Conspiracy.* San Francisco, CA.: Harper, 1997. 140.

churches do indeed work with the same precision as Jacob's Well. This point is remarkably well illustrated by a particular theology I asked Pastor Keel to formulate.

"BELONG—BEHAVE—BELIEVE"

I had looked forward to asking Pastor Keel about an interview, I read several years ago, concerning Jacob's Well's impact on Kansas City in a particular issue of *Christianity Today*. In the interview, Tim reflected on reversing the common pattern most evangelical churches follow of "believe-behave-belong" to "belong-behave-believe"—*How does this work as a theology?*

The reversal of the common evangelical pattern—"believe-behave-belong"—mirrors more accurately Jesus' ministry. The reversal—"belong-behave-believe"—is sociologically more accurate regarding Jesus' attention to his flock, according to Tim.

Once Jesus enters human history proclaiming, "The kingdom of God has come near, repent, and believe the good news!" (Mk. 1:15), he begins to drive malignant spirits out of tormented human beings, healing many of their infirmities and creating party atmospheres among the outcasts—"In that day they will say, 'Surely this is our God; we trusted in him, and he saved us. This is the Lord, we trusted in him; let us rejoice and be glad in his salvation" (Isa. 25:9).

"Our God Reigns," what does it look like? The Pharisees envisioned the overthrow of their oppressors, in their historical context, this was Rome; the Sadducees envisioned national sovereignty under their political rule and the cynical Essenes separated themselves from socio-political life and waited for the flames of hell to swallow up everyone, and everything that was contrary to their view of the Torah and its relation to culture.

But Jesus' inaugural eschatology (Jesus' announcement of the last days) was calling people into his space to live and belong, "Come and see that the Lord is good!" If we picture an illustration of concentric circles, and the outer-most circle is under the control of the Pharisees' hierarchical leadership; there are boundaries, and entrance into the circle is restricted to believing as the Pharisees believe. But in the center circle, Jesus stands over the kingdom of God, and we don't know where the boundaries are; we are either moving towards Jesus or away from him.

Judas moved away, the Centurion, in whom Jesus had not seen such faith in all of Israel,

though formerly far away, came near—Israel failed to see that their corporate election as God's chosen people (Genesis 12:1-3) was a calling to service instead of privilege. But the Pharisees were obsessed with power; for them, the way to success was greater power.

Community socializes us, being in a loving community transforms us and inspires us to begin thinking about reality differently. Tim reflected on time he and his family spent in Australia and New Zealand. Ranches were very vast, and ranchers and farmers spent most of their working lives building fences to keep their herds within the boundaries—Ranchers and farmers expended significant amounts of money and time attempting to control their livestock.

But once they began focusing on wells, they stopped worrying about boundaries—

"Believe – Behave – Belong" is all about building fences, this is the way of the Pharisees; "Belong-Behave-Believe" is all about creating wells, this is the way of the kingdom of God, this is the way of Jesus.

Jacob's Well is a church that believes community transformation is all about creating wells, both metaphorically and literally. The story of the transformation of the Pokot Tribe in Kenya through the construction of actual wells is a story about boundless "abiding"!

BOUNDLESS ABIDING!

Jacob's Well's ever-growing root system reaches across the earth to City Harvest Ministries in Nairobi, Kenya, and the people of Asilong village in Pokot, Kenya, located in the northwestern part of the nation.[186]

In 2006, Pastor Edward Simuyu, a Kenyan pastor, shared with Pastor Keel that his church, City Harvest, in Nairobi was working among the Pokot people. The availability of clean water in much of Africa is more precious than rare metals. The Pokot Tribe is nomadic and for a long time, they have fought for access to clean water, food, and land. For most of their history, the Pokot have raided villages and killed other tribes' people; they have stolen livestock throughout Kenya. They have been feared as a notorious, violent people.

But this is the way they have survived. City Harvest Church has demonstrated great courage by missionally engaging the Pokot, and Jacob's Well welcomed the opportunity to partner with Harvest Church. An intimate relationship between Harvest Church and Jacob's Well "took root" in 2007 and the result has been an amazing transformation in the Pokot village of Asilong and surrounding areas in Kenya.

Through Jacob's Well's "Advent Conspiracy,"[187] team members from the church drilled four water wells in Asilong to provide the Pokot clean water. In 2008, a six-member team from Jacob's Well visited Kenya and joined Pastor Edward Simuyu. The Jacob's Well's team's discovery of the overwhelming need of fresh water resulted in the drilling of six additional

---

[186] Jacob's Well. https://www.jacobswellchurch.org/ WATCH/LISTEN. Downloaded: 09/22/2021.

[187] Jacob's Well seeks ways to give each year during Advent. Giving to designated projects is referred to as, "Advent Conspiracy." Through the Advent Conspiracy, Jacob's Well has funded many missional projects to include the building of the wells in Asilong. Ibid. Downloaded: 09/22/2021.

wells over the course of the following three years. The transformation of the Pokot in Asilong was amazing! They no longer had to travel on foot for hours, only to wait twelve more hours in line to draw water from a single well that served a massive area—"They no longer went blind for lack of water to clean their face and eyes, their children were no longer attacked by African killer bees for being the only source of water nearby." And the Pokot were able to raise healthy livestock, and women had time to attend church, because the wells provided by Jacob's Well enabled them to do their chores in a timely manner.

Children were then freed to attend elementary school because they no longer had to walk to and from distant wells every day. And the Pokot no longer violently raided other villages as means to survive. And villagers in the surrounding Kenyan area no longer had to live in fear of the Pokot!

In November 2010, four team-members travelled to the Pokot region and with Pastor Edward, and the chiefs and elders, they dedicated the ten wells. And in November 2011, a team of architects from Jacob's Well traveled to Asilong to design and prepare to fund a secondary school. Jacob's Well's architectural team's planning has resulted in the construction of Asilong Christian High School.

The weapons we fight with are not the weapons of the world. On the contrary, they have divine power to demolish strongholds" (2 Cor. 10:4)—Abiding involves the integration of wisdom and, in this case, the transformation of a hostile, violent people, through the power of the Gospel setting free a community, rooted in the Vine and "living now like everyone will in the future"!

Pastor Tim acknowledged that Jesus is very precise regarding the language he uses, for example, he consistently speaks of the "Father," instead of God; "What is the Father like," "I know my Father," "Our Father in heaven"—*"The Person and life of Jesus informs the terms (the language) we use at Jacob's Well."* With this qualification in mind, Pastor Tim addressed my question regarding missional theology.

MISSIONAL THEOLOGY

I asked Pastor Tim about the name of his church, "Jacob's Well" and how it was particularly nuanced regarding missional theology?"

As above-mentioned, Pastor Keel is very intentional—Tim's intentionality is rooted in well-defined, theological reflection and framed in mission. Missional is a helpful framework for Pastor Keel's theology of mission—"Mission is the way in which we engage our community and even ourselves."

Mission is at the heart of everything—worship, preaching, prayer, justice .... And "everything" is at the heart of mission. According to Pastor Keel, the relationship of church and mission is a triad—e.g., *Kairos,* quality of time, that is, theological time, creativity, artistic life, in a word, worship; *Koinonia,* fellowship, spiritual formation, "congregations within the church" (small groups), family, children, and youth; and *Kronos,* quantity time, e.g., financial, facilities, stewardship, the Senior Leadership Team, *all flow out of mission.*

Tim continued by informing me about his "Kingdom Vision." (N.T. Wright has shaped Pastor Keel's Kingdom Vision in significant ways). First century Jewish language (historically, this was Second Temple Judaism) spoke of the present age they were living in as life "outside the garden," the world was oppressive, it was under Gentile rule. God gave the Torah to Israel, but the Jewish Nation strayed from it. God sent prophets calling on Israel to repent and pointing to the Age to Come, the Kingdom of Heaven, "God's Reign." Heaven is not a location but a reality—the reality of heaven and earth, the present age, and the future age, come together.

The entering of human history by Incarnate Deity, Jesus Christ, results in the reality of the Kingdom of Heaven being centered in God's Messiah—Yahweh has returned to renew the covenant! God's reign is now in effect in Jesus.

Paul talks about "citizens of heaven" (Phil. 3:20) who continue to "work out [their] salvation" (Phil. 2:12b-13); the kingdom of God includes the church, but the church is not the kingdom of God—"Church is people who behave in the present in a way that everyone will behave in the future."[188] Tim then added James 1:22—Christians behave in a way that they do not merely listen to the word, and so deceive themselves, [but they] do what it says." In this way, the church abides together in Christ and out of that, they demonstrate their intimate connection to the vine, both corporately and individually to the world (the "world" is a system that sets itself up against the reign of God, the world is defiant towards the reign of God).

Tim asserted that when he looks at the present age, he sees it saturated with the age to come; he teaches his congregation to behave in relation to the kingdom to come. First the Temple was the space between the present age and the age to come, then Jesus and now the church—the church is the "new Israel," this identity is related to the coming kingdom. As I listened to Tim Keel, I recalled N.T. Wright's words regarding the present church: "What Jesus was to Israel, the church must be for the world"[189]

---

[188] N.T. Wright, *Jesus and the Victory of God*, 643, states: The early church's unique understanding of the time of the End results in the disciple seeing "an underlying continuity between present bodily life and future bodily life, and that gives meaning and direction to present Christian living." The significance of Wright's biblical wisdom has prompted by understanding: *Our daily lives are conditioned by both our connection to Jesus' historical resurrection and our future imperishable, immortal and incorruptible resurrection and that is the source of ultimate meaning for every ordinary day of our lives* (cf. Rom. 4:25/1Cor. 15:42-58).

[189] N.T. Wright. *The Challenge of Jesus*. 181.

A robust missional theology involves the church, and individual Christians, standing in the space where the present age and the future age come together. The church, and individual believers must take a missionary posture in the community and proclaim the Gospel in such a way that they demonstrate its relevance as public truth—*The intimate connection of the church to the vine is made evident to the community through Christian compassion, justice, and the transforming power of the Gospel.*

A CLOSING REFLECTION

My final question for Pastor Keel was introduced by a statement: "I realize there is theological diversity (nuance) in the Emergent Movement. How do you see Jesus' "Kingdom Vision"?

Tim responded by saying that although he was formerly identified with the Emergent Movement, he has not publicly identified with it since 2009. Tim continues to maintain close relationships with pastors and theologians associated with the Emergent Movement. But new seasons that God has transitioned him through has required change to include new identity language and delivery of the unchanging Gospel in an ever-changing environment at Jacob's Well, and Pastor Keel's midtown cultural context in Kansas City, MO., and the world.

CHAPTER 11

KALEO MISSIONAL COMMUNITIES

PORTLAND, OR

"Learning To Live Like Jesus Together"

Reading from the lectionary, Pastor Paul Hoffman renews the vision of Kaleo Missional Communities every other Sunday.[190] This is necessary because the vision "leaks" every two weeks, that is, the vision needs refocusing, readjustments, and recalibration in the face of rapid demographic changes, twists and turns in community rhythms and relentless shifts in family and individual dynamics in the turbulent cultural landscape of southeast Portland, Oregon.

---

[190] Interview: Pastor Paul Hoffman, [founder, elder] Kaleo Missional Communities, Portland, Oregon (website) Kaleo Missional Communities are a part of the SOMA family.

Missional communities incarnate God's grace, justice, and love in priest-like ways, the missional community stands between God and their neighborhood, community and nation and welcomes the spiritually exiled into the kingdom of God. The missional community engages incarnational mission with the intent of becoming all things to all people *"for the sake of the gospel,"* (1 Cor. 9:23).

Sunday AM services center on God's mission. As we enter the sphere of life God has entered ahead of us, we often encounter life "all at once," a kaleidoscopic display of experiences collides with our psyche—mission can be disorienting, confrontational and unpredictable.

These liminal circumstances are moments in which we see Jesus engage the world through us in ways that are new to us! Sunday AM service is a context for disciples to share their experiences on mission during the week; it is a time to share how God answered prayer, and how God worked in amazing ways through the life of the missional practitioner! It is a time for testimonies that glorify God and the introduction of new disciples to the congregation! Sunday AM is set-aside for celebration of the great things God has done t8hrough his people during the week. It is a time talk about the missional community's mission and vision and how God's people are making a difference in people's lives, neighborhoods, and the city! It is a time to gather around the Table and celebrate the Eucharist with unrestrained thanksgiving! Sunday morning is a time for the community to grow together in love, to celebrate communitas!

Sunday AM is a time for "one another"—A time to comfort one another (2 Cor. 13:11); Agree with one another (2 Cor. 13:11); Live in peace with one another (2 Cor. 13:11); Greet one another (2 Cor. 13:11); Bear one another's burdens—that is, confront sin together and share the burden of sin together (Gal. 6:2); Bear with one another (Eph. 4:2); Encourage one another (1 Thess. 5:11); Build one another up (1 Thess. 5:11); Stop grumbling against one another (Jas. 5:9); Repent of speaking evil against one another (Jas. 4:11) —Communitas is an environment for God's covenant people to come together in genuine Christian community.[191]

KALEO—A MISSIONAL CONGREGATION

Kaleo Communities is a missional congregation "Learning To Live Like Jesus Together"—Brad Watson clearly, simply states that a Missional Community "has three equal and codependent pursuits":

1. Grow in our love for God (Gospel Enjoyment).
2. Grow in our love for one another (Community).
3. Grow in our love to our neighbors and city (Mission).[192]

Pastor Hoffman prefers "missional communities" instead of "missional church" because "communities" are more decentralized than "church" in Western thinking. "Learning To Live Like Jesus Together," requires each Kaleo community to "live out its identities."

Disciples (missional practitioners) live out their "baptismal identity." Believers are baptized in the name of the Father, the Son, and the Holy Spirit. We are baptized in the name of the Father because we are the family of God. We are baptized in the name of the Son because we are servants of the King sent to serve the "least of these" as He served us. And we are baptized in the name of the Spirit because we are God's Spirit-empowered missionaries sent to declare the Good News to the world so that others might come to know Jesus and as disciples of Christ, Kaleo Missional

---

[191] Brad Watson. *Sent Together; How the Gospel Sends Leaders to Start Missional Communities.* Second Edition. GCD Books, com/Books, www.gcdiscipleship.com.
[192] Ibid. 44.

Communities make disciples, principally, through joining Jesus on mission together—"Whatever God does to us, He also intends to do through us."[193]

Missional practitioners are then connected to "Gospel Purposes"—"They've been saved for a purpose,"[194] God intends to engage the city, the nation, and the world through them. And thirdly, "Gospel Practices" is a phase in which missional practitioners witness the Gospel "informing the everyday rhythms of life."[195] Pastor Hoffman refers to "Gospel Fluency," in relating how missional practitioners begin to live their lives in a way that every part of their lives (e.g., eating, celebrating, resting, working, playing) is "informed" and "reinforced" by the Gospel—Gospel Fluency enables missional practitioners to "Live with Gospel intentionality." [196]

Consequently, "All of life is mission" —Believers are always on mission, explains Pastor Hoffman. Whereas Philip, Peter and John were on "proactive common mission," that is, a group of missional practitioners sent on mission together to a particular people group, with a clearly defined mission ("proactive common mission" is when disciplemaking is most effective); "reactive" mission involves all of life, all the time.

The individual missional practitioner is making disciples wherever they are by modeling the life of Christ as Paul did, before both enemies of the Gospel (cf. Acts 23:1) and believers whom he [Paul] was shaping into dynamic disciples (cf. Acts 20:18, and 1 Cor. 11:1). Like Paul, all believers are to be imitators of Christ by following "God's example … as loved children and [walking] in the way of love, just as Christ loved us and gave

---

[193] Jeff Vanderstelt. "Baptismal Identity," Baptismal Identity Jeff Vanderstelt HD - YouTube. Downloaded: 02/06/2021.

[194] Jeff Vanderstelt. "How to Equip a Missional Community Series Sample/ How to Form a Missional Community/Soma. https://www.youtube.com/watch?v=ufPjFq66_OU&t=731s. Downloaded: 02/06/2021.

[195] Ibid.

[196] Ibid.

himself up for us as a fragrant offering and sacrifice to God" (Ephesians 5:1-2)—*How are you known by other people? What is your identity before a watching world, are you identified by your political party of choice, your indifference towards others, or your love for Jesus Christ?*

Regarding proactive common mission, how does Pastor Hoffman lead his missional community leaders in selecting a specific people group, organization, or school to serve? Pastor Hoffman referred to his adaptation of Brad Watson's "grid" for the purpose of incarnating common (proactive) mission in his book, *Sent Together.*[197]

Pastor Hoffman's wisdom, and love for Portland, is reflected in both his adaptation of Watson's "grid" and his effective application of it. In the Kaleo Communities missional context, the group selected is first determined by *proximity*—"Who is my neighbor?"—"Who lives near me? Who lives around me? Secondly, selecting a group involves *affinity*—"What are the interests of people around us? "Affinity feeds proximity." And thirdly, *cause*—"What can we do to serve these people, this organization or school for Christ?"

Kaleo Missional Communities' selection of a particular group is significantly influenced for by proximity, affinity, and cause. But the third layer of the process, *Cause*, is the "weightiest" —The missional community must know the people the Spirit has called them to, they must build relationships, build family. We must "love our enemies," stresses Paul Hoffman—and understand from the group themselves, what they are seeking; and what, in their view, are their needs?

To "love our enemies" is both a wise and effective [necessary] approach to contemporary Western culture. Kaleo Missional Communities is in a

---

[197] Brad Watson. *Sent Together.* 73-77. Watson establishes three broad categories for common missions: A Neighborhood as Common Mission, A Network as Common Mission, and A People as Common Mission.

season of shepherding people who have formerly feared the church, they have seen the church as a dangerous enemy—the politically charged cultural air in the West is extremely toxic and emotionally persuasive—and consequently, the church is viewed as a threatening, imperialistic political force driven by a quest for political power and a consequent determination to marginalize those that are "outside."

Kaleo connects with these people, who formerly saw themselves as antagonized by the church. Kaleo not only tells them who Jesus is, but more, they demonstrate who Jesus really is—*Note the kingdom-oriented ways.* Rather than seeing people as a mission to be achieved, they are centered on integrating their former enemies into covenant relationship in the context of community. *Mission is an outgrowth of the transformation, or if you will, transfiguration of the new man, instead of an end-in-itself.*

"The allure of chasing cultural-political moments flow both to the left and right." Pastor Hoffman cautions the missional congregation not to abandon relational promises they have made with underserved groups to pursue other groups who happen to be highlighted in the news cycle.

"A church must consider its role in bringing the kingdom to bear in any cultural moment but should be careful not to abandon their relational promises, a missional congregation must know its capacity; it's capacity to sustain relational commitments and capacity to expand them."

Knowing the needs of any group requires spending time with them, listening to their hearts and becoming a part of their group—How can a Kaleo Community become "all things" to the group, organization, or school, towards effectively serving the group? That is, *effectively* making disciples, through word and deed.[198]

---

[198] Ibid. 73.

Every believer on mission has a role critical to mission outcomes. Pastor Hoffman referred to Jeff Vanderstelt's illustration of "Building Missional Communities," through serving, for example, a high school football team. How would a missional team made up of a variety of people with diverse backgrounds; some know a lot about football, and others know almost nothing about the game, but what they share in-common is a desire to serve the needs of young men on a high school football team through means of Christian charity.

An example of a typical inner-city Portland high school football team includes racially diversified players. They are majority black and white players, they (black and white players together), in an inner-city setting, commonly live in a marginalized community, their families are poor.

The missional team must first learn what are the needs of the players; they must become acquainted with the players and develop relationship with them and their families—The intentions of the missional team must be clear. Some members of the missional team will assist the coaches (or perhaps, coach themselves); other team members will fund-raise for equipment, and personal clothing needs. Other team members will provide stadium repairs, maintenance, and upkeep. And members will do laundry and prepare food—Sometimes, a large buffet following a game, other times, a meal with families in the church or delivering meals to the player's homes. Other times, snacks during practice and games. And still other team members with flexible schedules will attend all games and support the team as a recognizable fan by the players. Special mementos, and awards will be given to players for their outstanding performance at the end of the season (imagine the defensive lineman of the year being awarded an Aaron Donald jersey!).[199] *Joining Jesus on his mission requires every member of the mission team to participate in a vital way.*

THE MISSIONAL CONGREGATION AND THE SOCIO-POLITICAL DIVIDE

I asked Pastor Hoffman, "How do you see the role of the missional congregation in relation to Western Civilization's present socio-cultural and political divide?" Paul stressed the critical role of an identity theology—*What does it mean to be Christian in the early 21st century West? How should we live in these unpredictable times? What does God require of me?*

In understanding what it means to follow Jesus, the Table is the only thing big enough to bridge the divide—John 13:34: *"A new command I give you: Love one another. As I have loved you, so you must love one another. ^{35}By this everyone will know that you are my disciples if you love one another."* Missional congregations must seek out and partner with people formerly repelled by the church—The critical need to love our enemies involves building "wells" for the thirsty, not "corrals" for our enemies.

---

[199] Aaron Donald is a Defensive Player of the Year in the NFL and Hall-Of-Fame bound defensive tackle for the Los Angeles Rams.

CHAPTER 12

DOXA CHURCH

BELLEVUE, WA.

"Doxa Church exists to see the Eastside and beyond saturated with the glory of God in the everyday stuff of life. This requires the presence of Christ in his people, living as disciples who make disciples of Jesus."

Adam Hillyer, with his wife, Sunnee, serve Jesus in the San Francisco Bay Area as the Director of Saturate, a SOMA Church mission committed to seeing a Gospel saturation movement happen in North America and beyond.[200]

---

[200] SOMA. Saturate Equipping. https://wearesoma.com/saturate-equipping/. Downloaded: 06/04/2021. SOMA is a family of missional community churches committed to disciple-making toward "gospel saturation." Saturate exists to catalyze, equip, and unite the global church toward missional living, everyday discipleship, and gospel fluency.

Prior to moving to San Francisco, Adam was the Director of Missional Communities at DOXA, Bellevue, Washington.[201] My interview with Adam primarily focuses on his former role as the Director of Missional Communities at DOXA.

DOXA was formed in 2015 with the primary purpose of living out the story of Jesus Christ in "the everyday stuff of life." DOXA's passion is for disciples to make disciples, to this end, believers see themselves as missionaries in every part of life, everyday—*DOXA disciples live as a sent people.*

I asked Adam to elaborate on DOXA's mission statement: "Being on mission to reach the Eastside [Bellevue is east of Seattle] in the everyday stuff of life." DOXA sees themselves as missionary teams, proactively involved together for mission to specific people groups and/or a team of missionaries, individually committed to every day, every moment (reactive) mission. In practical terms, DOXA's missional practitioners daily enter the rhythms of life with "mission in common" or "common mission."

What are the broad contours in how you equip people for lives of purpose and training them to follow Jesus? A first order concern involves motivation—DOXA's narrative emphasizes engaging Jesus through missional, spiritual practice over a pursuit of a lot of Bible knowledge as means to disciple-making. DOXA's missional ecclesiology emphasizes a "discipleship pathway."

The discipleship pathway begins with the joining of a DNA Group (3-4 people of the same gender). DNA groups discover truth about God, nurture matters of the heart, and act in response to God's work. The practitioner's identity in Christ is formed—*The Jesus story is lived out as their story.*

---

[201] SOMA views a missional community as "a family of missionary servants sent to make disciples that make disciples in the everyday stuff of life." And towards this end, SOMA's highly successful missional model for training, "*We make Disciples and Plant Churches of Missional Communities Towards Gospel Saturation,*" has well prepared missional practitioners throughout the United States.

In their journey together, missional communities require accountability to one another throughout—Coaches lead missional communities through modeling the "rule of life" on mission. Coaches emphasize four spiritual foundations: "Life with God," the practitioner's personal life in Christ is emphasized; "Life in community" the practitioner's love for people different from them is emphasized; "Life on life" emphasizes transparent spiritual friendship and "Life on mission" focuses on making disciples by living as a people sent and evangelizing the lost.

Adam offered an example of modeling life on mission, "partnering with apartment life." A couple in a missional community moves into an apartment and connects with people living in the apartment community.

The couple seeks out those new to the apartments and invites them to a welcome party attended by people living in the apartments. The missional couple connects with the apartment community as they begin learning people's story at a bar-b-que—Sharing in a meal together is a means of connection modeled by Jesus.[202]

Gospel fluency is all about connecting the Gospel to people's stories and introducing them to Jesus Christ—The missional couple is not only modeling disciple-making for practitioners in their missional community, but also for not-yet disciples in the apartment complex.

"SATURATE THE SOUND"

Adam continued by explaining how Saturate the Sound brings together pastors from different denominations committed to seeing a "Gospel Saturation Movement" throughout the Puget Sound Area (Seattle and the

---

[202] See my book, *Following Jesus to Burning Man, Recovering the Church's Vocation.* (Hamilton Books, 2011). Chapter Two: "A Glutton and a Drunkard" is a thorough study of the meals of Jesus.

greater metropolitan area, and Tacoma, and Olympia and several small communities).[203]

A brief video on the "Saturate the Sound" website begins with the narrator proclaiming, "God has a new song for the Sound."[204] This proclamation points to an astounding vision for residents of the Puget Sound Area.

The vision of Saturate the Sound is to see every man, woman and child have a daily encounter with Jesus where they live, work, learn and play—"We know this will require new churches, and church renewals. It will require every disciple and church working together."[205]

Every church must be committed to making disciples—Every church is called to equip a "gospel-fluent community on mission making disciples of Jesus in every neighborhood."[206] And further, believers are "identified in every key business sector, company, and government trained context and supported as missionaries in the workplace."[207] Additionally, "communities on mission,"[208] are united by the gospel "in every elementary, middle school, high school, and college"[209] in the Puget Sound. Finally, pastors are committed to seeing "every recreational sphere saturated with Jesus's people on mission"[210]—"This is how Jesus transforms the Puget Sound."[211]

---

[203] Adam's and Sunnee's mission in San Francisco involve their participation in the Bay Area's "Saturate San Francisco."
[204] SATURATE THE SOUND. "The World Waits for Followers of Jesus to be Authentic and Inspiring." https://www.saturatethesound.com/. Downloaded: 06/11/2021.
[205] Ibid.
[206] Ibid.
[207] Ibid.
[208] Ibid.
[209] Ibid.
[210] Ibid.
[211] Ibid.

Towards this end, pastors are divided into cohorts consisting of 8–10 leaders. Cohorts view and discuss several videos together, e.g., "Environments Necessary for Disciple-Making," "Life with God in Community," "Life on Mission—Making Disciples," "Community—Loving People Different from Us," "Foundations for Making Disciples—Living as a Sent People," etc.

Adam's concluding remarks were his response to my question, "How do you see the role of the Missional Church in relation to Western Civilization's present socio-cultural and political divide? By implication, a commitment to Gospel Saturation throughout the United States places the Missional Church in a position that all churches ought to occupy, they don't choose sides in the present social-cultural and political divide. To the contrary, missional congregations bring political enemies together to serve a purpose much greater than anything the socio-political world can offer—"The power of the Gospel brings people together in community." This serves as a powerful apologetic for the Christian faith to the watching world.

CHAPTER 13

MADE TO FLOURISH

OVERLAND PARK, KANSAS

> "*We empower pastors and their churches to integrate faith, work, and economic wisdom for the flourishing of their communities.*"[212]

I opened my interview with Dr. Charlie Self, the former Director of City Development and now an advisor and contributor for Made to Flourish, by asking him a question prompted by a statement on the Made to Flourish website: "When you speak of 'closing the gap between Sunday and Monday,' how and in what ways, is disciple-making implicated?" In short, please elaborate on "discipleship pathways."

---

[212] Made to Flourish: https://www.madetoflourish.org/ Downloaded: 04/05/2019

The "gap" between Sunday and Monday refers to modernism's sacred/secular dichotomy.[213] With subtle influences emanating from a sacred/secular view of reality in mind, Dr. Self often asks Christians on Sunday morning, "How will you worship God tomorrow?"

Many (refreshingly) reply in missionally reflective ways, "I run a dry cleaner and that has meaning to God"—Work has inherent value as well as instrumental value as perceived through the lens of a kingdom worldview.

We must see the narrative of Scripture as a whole—We need to discover what we were made to do. According to Genesis 1-2, we were created to dwell in God's presence and do his work in the world. And Revelation 21-22 echoes and expands this as God dwells with his people and all the nations bring the fruits of their redeemed labor to the Holy City.

We can also connect the immanent and economic Trinity as we work. Our identity and value are always more than our current jobs, just as Father, Son, and Holy Spirit dwell in a mutual delight of love, holiness, and unity. Yet we are called to carry out our mission…and God's activity as Sender (the Father), Sent One (the Son), and Sanctifier (The Holy Spirit) offer rich resources for daily work. Local churches can equip entrepreneurs and incubate new businesses and economic initiatives, becoming catalysts for economic transformation. Our assets are our members and their missionally-driven lives throughout the week—Work and mission are inseparable. Charlie added, "Part of being fully human is working"—*and We know God through His works.*

FLORISHING CHURCHES

---

[213] Dorothy Sayers. "The Secular Vocation is Sacred, Serve God in Your Profession, Not Outside It." (Please Chapter 2, "Living Missionally," Subtitle: Stage 1: "Challenging Nest-Bound Believers" for an expanded explanation of Sayers' point).

Flourishing results when churches have clarity and creativity in their unique missions, collaborate with other churches. New networks are formed, and pastors gather to share ideas, best practices, and enjoy relationships that result in initiatives that make a difference in all domains of influence. We need to think about outcomes, not programs. And we need to ask ourselves, "What does a healthy disciple look like?" "Discipleship," insists Dr. Self, "includes all dimensions of the human person and all domains of society." A great resource for this revolution from programs to outcomes is found at www.discipleshipdynamics.com.

But an underlying frustration persists for many pastors regarding how disciple-making is done today. When asked how they disciple their congregation, many pastors still point to small groups that come together and grow and mature in Christ through Bible study, prayer, and fellowship. Although there is nothing wrong with Bible study, prayer, and fellowship in a small group context, what does this look like on a Tuesday afternoon in the workplace, at public events, and community life in general?

There is a difference between outcomes—Character growth, praying without ceasing, caring about the marginalized, and outputs or programs—how many small groups a church has, how many volunteered for a mission's trip or how many signed up for the Christmas program. *Disciple-making concentrates on our need to ensure that our programs serve outcomes.*

DISCIPLESHIP DYNAMICS—*DISCOVER, DEFINE, DISCIPLE*

"What the world needs now is Jesus and a good job"—John Perkins

Dr. Self, through collaboration with other colleagues, developed a Discipleship Dynamics Assessment.[214] The assessment provides a "clear and descriptive evaluation of each individual's personal level of Christian discipleship."[215] Five dimensions are assessed, and thirty-five Biblical discipleship outcomes are evaluated. The five dimensions of the assessment are as follows:

- **Spiritual Formation**—In this first dimension, the assessment identifies eight outcomes "indicative of the disciple's level of spiritual formation."[216]
- **Personal Wholeness**—The second dimension focuses on issues that reveal the level of our emotional health.[217] Eight outcomes deal with personal wholeness from the Scriptures.
- **Healthy Relationships**—In this dimension, the Scriptures shed light on "the practical expressions of 'love your neighbor as yourself.'"[218] Eight outcomes from the Scriptures deal with the disciple's relational health.
- **Vocational Clarity**—The fourth dimension observes that the clergy are not alone in their calling, every follower of Jesus Christ has received a "calling" to serve God and humankind. Seven outcomes Biblically formulated source an examination of the disciple's vocational clarity.
- **Economics and Work**—The fifth of the discipleship dimensions argues that "the workplace and participation in the economy is the

---

[214] Discipleship Dynamics LLC. *Discover, Define, Disciple.* Springfield, MO. 4319 S. National #207, 65810. https://discipleshipdynamics.com/about-the-assessment/#economics-work. Downloaded: 10/19/2021.
[215] Ibid.
[216] Ibid.
[217] Ibid. (Paraphrase, instead of a direct quote).
[218] Ibid.

context wherein we live out The Great Commission (Mt. 28:18-20; Acts 1:8), the Great Commandment (Mt. 22:37-40) and our personal mission (Eph. 2:10)."[219] The assessment identifies six discipleship outcomes in this dimension.

Reaching unchurched and de-churched people in various cultural contexts requires every local pastor to be a global missionary. Professor Self continued, "We need an incarnational apologetic linked with evangelism and integrated with spiritual vitality, systemic justice, and personal transformation."

Do we have the character and competencies to adjust to our pastoral vocation? The Discipleship Dynamic Assessment developed by Dr. Charlie Self and others is an invaluable aid in not only evaluating our character and competency for the work of the ministry but as well, it is designed to enable us to capitalize on our strengths and develop confidence in our weaknesses.

Chapter 12, Made to Flourish, seamlessly transitions to Chapter 13—The exceptional couple that pastors the next church flourish in ways that demonstrates the effectiveness of the Made to Flourish discipleship model. This husband-and-wife team is together a rare example of apostolic-like faith, seemingly boundless imagination, and entrepreneurial insight, innovation, and wisdom.

---

[219] Ibid.

CHAPTER 14

VICTORY CHURCH

YORKTOWN, VA

"Discover What Faith Can Do"

Jamé Bolds began his career at the Acton Institute for the Study of Religion and Liberty, an educational research institute i.e., "a think-tank." Acton's mission is "to promote a free and virtuous society characterized by individual liberty and sustained religious principles."[220] Acton's core principles involve the integration of "Judeo-Christian Truths with Free Market Principles." "Economic Liberty" and "Economic Value" are among the core principles that Jamé has brought to pastoral ministry.[221]

Jennifer Bolds is a Marriage & Family Therapist and professional musician. Jennifer works as corporate consultant teaching engineers and sci-

---

[220] Acton Institute: "Our Mission & Core Principles." https://www.acton.org/about/mission. Downloaded: 10/27/2021.
[221] Pastor Bolds's PhD dissertation integrates theology and economics.

entists how to be emotionally intelligent (i.e., recognizing how they are "wired" and motivated) as a practical skill set.

GOD'S ALL-SURPASSING GRACE!

Jamé and Jennifer Bolds were elected pastors of Victory Church in 2013. The church had 28 people, it had less than $10,000 in the bank, and it was in-debt 1.3 million dollars. The preschool was broke, and the building where the church gathers looked like it had not been updated since the early 2,000's and the by-laws weren't touched since "Acts 2"! And although the name appeared to be "anything but," Jamé and Jennifer believed the Lord called them to "Victory Church."

By God's all-surpassing grace, Victory Church witnessed a miracle involving a 4.5 million dollar turn-around in only 5 years! The pre-school has a waiting list, the buildings (both the church and the preschool) are completely updated, the church has an endowment, a new 100-unit retirement community (one of three LLC's), 46 acres of land stretching into two counties and absolutely no debt—Victory Church is flourishing!

Jame and Jennifer are now in their 8th year as pastors of Victory Church; by the time they celebrate their 10th anniversary, the church will have in place an "economic model at a reverse tithe" —*The church will give 90% of their income and keep 10%*! Like virtually every-other church, Victory Church has had to navigate the challenging conditions caused by COVID, but great is God's faithfulness, the pandemic cannot resist His providential purposes!

DISCOVERING JESUS IN EVERYDAY LIFE

Regards Victory Church's Mission, *"We invite people to Discover Jesus in everyday life,"* I asked Pastor Bolds to expound on Victory Church's Mission.

Pastor Jamé began by asserting that he is obsessed by the question: "What kind of disciples is Victory producing?"

At Victory Church, disciples are called "Victors"—What does a disciple look like after being at Victory for 2 years? Johan Mostert, Charlie Self, and Pastor Bolds are partners in helping leaders effectively use the Discipleship Dynamics Assessment.[222]

Charlie Self stresses, "What does a disciple look like?" Pastor Bolds' "obsession" is quantified in Victory's brand: "Discover what faith can do"—"We think about Spiritual Formation—*Discover Jesus,* Personal Wholeness—*Discover Myself,* Healthy Relationships—*Discover Others,* Vocational Clarity—*Discover Purpose,* and Economics & Work—*Discover Work.*"

Discipleship is not an outcome, its not about programs. We [the contemporary North American Church] produce churches that produce Sunday morning attendance. But what does a believer's faith look like on Monday, not Sunday? Jamé contended that he is constantly addressing the heresy of the Sunday/Monday divide. Pastor Bolds seeks to disciple people for Monday morning, not Sunday morning. People become disciples at work, beginning on Monday, that's where most of their life is lived.

Discipleship is about a profound question: "Where is God at work?"—Metaphorically and practically? So, we see this compound question as a mission, a Gospel proclamation: 1. Are we inviting people? 2. Are we discovering Jesus? 3. Is it in everyday life? "We invite people to discover Jesus in everyday life … that becomes our text for everything we do."

How we work this out in the congregation is in practical ways. Sunday School and Small Groups are important, but when you are making disciples, you are concentrating on what it looks like in Personal Formation, Personal

---

[222] Discipleship Dynamics. Coaching and Consulting. https://discipleshipdynamics.com/coaching-and-consulting/. Downloaded: 10/27/2021.

Wholeness, Personal Relationships, Personal Vocation and Personal Work and Economics—*Do "Victors" look at their work as a way of creating value for other people?* At Victory Church, there is no distinction, no separation, between sacred and secular—*"Everything is sacred: Marriage, parenting, work, the way we conduct business ... everything is sacred."*

ADDING VALUE TO YOUR COMMUNITY

How does Victory Church's DNA work-itself out through your congregation? We have a preschool, and we provide 18 jobs for high school educated women, young mothers. If they are with us for 3 months, we pay for their early-childhood credential (we pay for the education they need to teach in our preschool). "We provide a discount on child-care; we undercut the market by an average of 40% (In the Virginia Commonwealth, daycare averages $1,200.00 a month. We charge $800.00 monthly)." "We paid our teachers during the required COVID quarantines."

Because we do that for our teachers, we create an economic effect; they can more easily pay rent, buy clothes, food, and other necessities. As a consultant, Jame asks churches: "How do you add value to your community? Churches typically answer, "We have a clothes closet" and/or "a food pantry." The presumption is, the local Boy Scouts group or Awanas Club will pick up the slack—some "do-gooder" organization will pick up the slack. But "What is unique about your church?"

Pastor Bolds continued, saying, "We have a partnership with the YMCA. We converted part of our property into soccer fields; we can provide youth-sports for little or no cost to families. We have contracted with a development company to build a retirement community on our property, and we offer long-term retirement care at a fraction of the costs in other similar communities. *Indeed, if Victory Church were to close, there would be a gap from cradle to grave in the community.*

When you apply economic wisdom to church life, you bless people practically. An example of this is if your baby is with us from the nursery to graduation from preschool, we will give you a $1,000.00 scholarship to go into a 4-year old's college fund. This benefit is in-place through an agreement with Thrivent Financial in Minneapolis, Minnesota.

Jennifer Bolds does marriage and family therapy for a fraction of the cost based on a sliding scale related to personal income. How does your church add value to your community?

When Pastor Jamé was on PhD sabbatical, Pastor Jennifer and the Church Board decided to pay for all the back-to-school supplies for the elementary school in the city. What is the social and economic value your church brings to the community? If your church closed, how would the community be affected? How do you structure your church, so it never runs out of money?

Pastors need to realize that they are not only pastoring a church, but they are also pastoring a zip code—Are you imbedded in the life of your community? Do you know the City Manager? How do you help the business community?

All of this comes out of a "theology of the city." In 605 BC, the prophet Jeremiah wrote a letter to the surviving elders, and all other Jewish people (to include Daniel the prophet) who had been carried into exile from Jerusalem to Babylon by Nebuchadnezzar.[223]

> *This is what the Lord Almighty, the God of Israel, says to all those I carried into exile from Jerusalem to Babylon: "Build houses and settle down; plant gardens and eat what they produce. Marry and have sons and daughters; find wives for your sons and give your daughters in marriage, so that they*

---

[223] The Assyrians left Jerusalem in ruin following their invasion.

too may have sons and daughters. Increase in number there; do not decrease. Also, seek the peace and prosperity of the city to which I have carried you into exile. Pray to the Lord for it, because if it prospers, you too will prosper" (Jer. 29:4-7).

The Hebrew term translated "prosperity" (*shālēm*) is a derivative of the Old Testament theological term translated "peace" (*shālōm*).[224] The root meaning of the verb *shālēm* expresses the true meaning of *shālōm*: "Completeness, wholeness, harmony, fulfillment is closer to the meaning."[225] Implicit in the understanding of the term *shālēm* is "unimpaired relationships with others and fulfillment in one's undertakings."[226]

God's covenant people were to seek the "peace" and "prosperity" of Babylon—*That's what God calls us to do, the only way we prosper, is if our city prospers.* We plant gardens, we create value. We multiply and we work for peace, justice, mercy, and flourishing—*We work for our city's peace and prosperity; we bring shalom to our city. We become a meaningful part of the city; there is no difference between the sacred and the secular.*

In closing, I asked Pastor Bolds how Victory Church's programs, e.g., mission's trips, small groups, "Kids & Families," "Rooted Students," and Victory Preschool serve Victory Church's outcomes, specifically, the church's vision.

Pastor Bolds answered my question with an example. Jamé reflected on some teenagers who recently went to Summer Camp. One of the teenagers wants to be a medical doctor but after going to Camp, she wanted to be a missionary. Pastor Jamé encouraged her to expand her vision to include both a calling to missions and medicine. "You could go to med-school,"

---

[224] R. Laird Harris, Gleason L. Archer, Jr., Bruce K. Waltke. *Theological Wordbook of the Old Testament.* Vol. 2. Chicago, IL: Moody Press, 1980, entry 2401, 931.
[225] Ibid.
[226] Ibid.

said Pastor Jamé, and "instead of spending summers at your beach house in Jamaica, you could give your life away on the margins, as a missionary doctor. Eventually, you could end-up full-time as a missionary doctor." Jamé stressed a Biblical principle with the bright, young student: "It's never either/or but rather, always both/and with God."

CHAPTER 15

GREENHOUSE CHURCH

GAINSVILLE, FL.

"WE SEE"—*"Churches of real disciples; not part-time believers… People that love God as Father, follow Him as Rabbi, and honor Him as King… People that give themselves for one another and the cause of the lost and the least"*

Regarding select missional congregations, my interview with Matt Ulrich, Microchurch Pastor, Greenhouse Church, is a fitting "bookend" to my first interview (Chapter 8) with Tomy Wilkerson, Director, The Underground Network, Tampa, Florida. The ecclesia model employed by both churches is the same, regarding structure, but Greenhouse uniquely and intentionally (on multi-levels) sees itself as a "both/and" church—This distinction is integral to an understanding of the operations of Greenhouse especially the penultimate enterprise of disciplemaking.

My first question posed to Pastor Ulrich was, "How does Greenhouse Church's ecclesial model empower microchurches?" Greenhouse frames its model in an ecclesial hermeneutic reflected in the ancient church in Acts (2:42-47):

> *⁴² They devoted themselves to the apostles' teaching and to fellowship, to the breaking of bread and to prayer. ⁴³ Everyone was filled with awe at the many wonders and signs performed by the apostles. ⁴⁴ All the believers were together and had everything in common. ⁴⁵ They sold property and possessions to give to anyone who had need. ⁴⁶ Every day they continued to meet together in the temple courts. They broke bread in their homes and ate together with glad and sincere hearts, ⁴⁷ praising God and enjoying the favor of all the people. And the Lord added to their number daily those who were being saved.*

Acts 2:42-47 is one of the earliest and most pure descriptions of the church found in the New Testament—the church in Acts "met together, lived life together, not just in buildings, not just together on Sundays, not just in a church service," but they continually lived life together, in a radically authentic way in Jesus.

In this "raw, organic pursuit of Jesus," the early church developed "a bare-bone structure that has been successfully used throughout church history." Matt continued, "Their way of discipleship could be transferred and caught regardless of socio-political landscape, it was immune to backlash and persecution, and because they met in the Temple courts, and they broke bread in their homes." Acts 2:42-47 is a beautiful model of how the primitive church lived life together in the way of Jesus.

The church in Acts "worshiped together, they're on mission together, they're in community with one another, they're in the Temple but they're also in their homes. So public life and private life converge; there is a macro expression of church but there is also a micro expression as well." The early church was countercultural, and yet, beautiful in their way of doing church—"For us at Greenhouse, we're so moved by this depiction of the church that we have devoted ourselves to seeing this first century reality manifested in the twenty-first century church."

Matt stressed that Greenhouse also recognizes, "that it's not only structure that brings life, but the focus, and the love and the desperation for Jesus." Pastor Ulrich observed that the "American Church has tended to believe a 'Field of Dreams' type of thing that if you build, then they will come;' we don't believe that which is why we're not putting our trust in a building and programs, we're just trying to reconnect with the way the early church practiced radical life on life discipleship that ended up changing the world forever."

Greenhouse does not deemphasize the significance of Sunday morning gatherings, but to the contrary, "if lost people are hearing about Jesus, followers of Jesus are being refreshed, souls are being recalibrated, like, we're going to celebrate that." Greenhouse doesn't think that traditional weekend gatherings are a bad thing, "they just don't think they're the only thing"— "For us, faith is more than Sunday, discipleship isn't taught, it's caught, and Jesus told his disciples to follow him, and they did for three years."

Paul told his disciples to follow him as he followed Christ. The Apostle was not only referring to when the church came together in one place, but to all of life, every day. And in the same way, Greenhouse calls "people to be disciples of a 24/7 lifestyle because Sunday alone just is not going to 'cut it.'"

Greenhouse Church then takes a "both/and" approach to church life— "We believe that the macrochurch and weekend gatherings can do what the microchurch cannot, but we also believe that there are things that happen at the microchurch gathering which are crucial for real discipleship to take place that can't happen in the macrochurch gathering."

Pastor Ulrich concludes, "We believe that both these dimensions have a place in creating an authentic discipleship culture that captures the essence of the Acts 2 church. For us, a lot of what happens on Sunday, in the macrochurch context, creates culture, unity through vision, teaching, worship and harvest. And microchurches are that smaller weekly gathering where we cultivate a lifestyle of worship, mission, and community of being disciples and making disciples."

A both/and approach offers great teaching and worship on Sunday that is just not available in a microchurch context. But missiologically, America is still in a place where people will come to church. Some people will not come to my house, to meet with a small group of people, "but they will still come to church on a Sunday because there is a cultural ethos that even in this post-Christian generation people understand church going on Sunday, … is a place of harvest."

But there are also people who say, "I'm never going to church, but I will come to your house, and I will hear what you have to say there." So, at Greenhouse, "if we can utilize a Sunday morning to win souls and make disciples, we're going to do it. But we're also very aware that that is a deficient model of church by itself."

The "both/and," "macro/micro" approach enables Greenhouse to create multi-layered contexts for disciples to make disciples. On Sundays, everyone is made aware of microchurches in sermons, bulletin and digital/multimedia announcements, and a huge display occupies a large space in the lobby.

Matt stressed that virtually everyone knows about microchurches, and they acknowledge both the centralized significance of microchurches to the purpose of Greenhouse Church, and the decentralized culturally transformative power of microchurches for Gainesville, especially on the margins, among the disenfranchised, and the University of Florida community.

Pastor Ulrich asserts that, "We also leverage the momentum and the synergy of the Hub to help train microchurch leaders and disciplemakers; some have informal training in the micro- church context, but we also have a formal training that happens at the Hub. Our both/and approach enable us to "maximize our missional reach and helps us make disciples."

I noted, "You have related to a theology of microchurches in implicit ways in our interview but definitively, in the Greenhouse Church context, what is a theology of microchurches?" Greenhouse church follows the same model as the Underground "worship, mission, and community…." For Greenhouse, a microchurch theology is rooted in Acts 2:42-47, but it is also in Ephesians 4:1; 11-15—"Live a life worthy of the calling you have received."

The Greenhouse paradigm is to equip the saints for the work of the ministry—"We (the pastoral staff) at the Hub, are vocationally working at the church, but we are not the 'ministers,' rather, our calling is to equip the ministers to go and do the work of the ministry."

If someone comes up to me, as the microchurch pastor, and says to me, "I think the church should have an outreach to the homeless," my response would be, "That's great, when are you going to start?"—"No, …. I want the church…."—"You are the church; the church is not the building, the church is the people, you are the church. We will come alongside of you, and we will train you, and we will help you financially… So, if this is a passion God has given you, then let's build the church around that."

We are constantly asking our people, "What's the call that you have received?" "What is the things God has put on your heart? What is the passion, the desires, the angst that you have, the things that you find joy in?"

So, we have microchurches all over the place… We have one in the "Juvie Centers," we have a lady who does scrap booking; she has seen at a dozen people saved in her scrap booking microchurch. "There're all these microchurches that meet, and they are based around the passions, the callings, or even just the hobbies of people. We allow that to be the driving force behind what the microchurch is and what it looks like. As-long-as there is worship, mission and community and its reproducible we are OK with however that looks…."

Greenhouse's theology of microchurches is rooted deeply in Ephesians 4, "What's the call" "Let's build the church around that call …" And "the APEST" (4:11)—"We're really big on apostle, prophet, evangelist, shepherd, teacher as not just 'seats' in the church but we feel that every believer is equipped with one or more of the APESTs." "We really think that Church is expressed when the APESTs are fully functioning… Even with microchurches, is the APESTs present?"—"Do you have apostles that are starting things? Do you have prophets that are calling you back to the voice of the Lord? Evangelists who are bringing in new people? Shepherds taking care of the flock? Teachers teaching the Word? Ephesians is a big piece of our theology for microchurches." The following is a sampling of the nearly one-hundred diverse microchurches that serve, in transforming ways, Gainsville, and the greater metro-area.[227]

MICROCHURCHES

"CREATED. Gainesville"—"Created. Gainesville is committed to reaching and restoring lives impacted by sex trafficking and sexual exploitation within our community, state, and nationally."

COFFEE BREAK WITH BETTY—"Weekly time of refreshing to share God's word and pray together."

---

[227] GREENHOUSE MICROCHURCHES. https://greenhousechurch.org/connect/microchurches/. Downloaded: 01/24/2022.

CREATIVE PROCESS DISCIPLESHIP—"We believe life is a journey of finding Jesus in our daily lives, as we live to help people see Jesus's life and his light inside of them. Using the creative process to enhance Bible study, we engage in a fun and joyful adventure whereby our eyes may see the wonderful things in God's law."

DIVERSE MULTIGENERATIONAL DISCIPLES—"What does it mean to be a disciple of Jesus? Join us as we grow in deeper relationship with the Lord and be transformed by His love and the power of His Spirit in community!"

BICYCLE UNIVERSITY AND BIKE REPAIR—"The bicycle repair ministry is focused on providing reliable bicycle repair in the neighborhoods to those of all ages and to give away as many bicycles as God gives us. Our outreach is to carry on this service with the gospel explained and encouraged at every opportunity."

INTERNATIONAL OUTREACH THURSDAY FRIENDSHIP GROUP—"The goal of International Outreach Thursday Friendship Group is to share the love of Christ through missional discipleship with internationals by building authentic relationships, showing radical hospitality, and providing a safe place to have community."

ALACHUA REGIONAL JUVENILE DETENTION CENTER—"We go out to the juvenile detention center and preach, share, and minister to the boys and girls."

JOSE ORTEZE MEN'S GROUP—"Come and grow in the Lord with other men as we learn to walk in truth, victory, and discipleship."

OASIS—"Older Adults Still In Service"

RAWLINGS MENTORING—"Our newest school partnership is with Rawlings Elementary. Be a mentor to a 3rd - 5th grade student."

The SOCK MINISTRY—"Bringing the Poor and Needy together assuring that they feel cared for and well feed; we serve together in the City Hall Parking lot of Downtown Gainesville three times a week… Praying, Ministering the Word of God, giving them Hot Meals, Clothing, and Personal Hygiene Products that has been donated to us."

THE GREENHOUSE DISCIPLES' AND DISCIPLE-MAKERS' PATHWAY

"What does disciplemaking at the Greenhouse Church look like?" An Old Testament theology of discipleship commissioned everyone for spiritual reproduction—"Every family was responsible for disseminating the spiritual DNA of Israel to the next generation, leaders were raised up, and even if you were just a farmer, you were responsible, everyone played a part in reproducing spiritual truth, culture, and climate."

"So, for us, we feel the same way, you don't have to have a church of a thousand people to be a disciplemaker, you only need one person, your own child—We put that mandate on each of our members … You can't outsource this responsibility to the pastor as he preaches, you are a minister of the Gospel, you are responsible to fulfill the imperative of the Great Commission."

Pastor Ulrich stressed, "If you are here, at Greenhouse Church, you are expected to be pursuing the Lord in worship, pursuing mission, reaching the lost, and making disciples in a community with other disciples. And we rally around them in the microchurch context."

"Acts 2 is the formative ecclesial model, Eph. 4 is a lot of the 'drive-in' terms of why you need to be a part of this, and the overall thematic vision of discipleship and God's people making disciples" —Therefore, every member needs to commit to ministry in a microchurch.

Disciplemaking at Greenhouse Church begins with an overview and prepares the disciple to cultivate their own discipleship—The discipleship pathway begins with an overview of what a disciple is: A disciple is "a fully committed follower of Jesus who is progressing in worship, mission, and community."[228] "Living in the Green" is descriptive of a disciple at Greenhouse Church who is "progressing in worship, mission, and community." A disciple, "Living in the Green" is encouraged to follow a discipleship pathway—Disciple-Makers know what they are doing (*definition*), Where they are going (*pathway*), and what it takes to get there (*essentials*).[229]

Greenhouse Church's Discipleship Pathway consists of five stages:[230]

The Path: New Connection → Interested → Believer → Disciple → Disciple-Maker

Defining The Who:

- New Connection: Build a relationship, have intentional conversation.
- Interested: Gauge their beliefs/Pre-salvation Discipleship/Share Gospel.
- Believer: Begin Discipleship Training; join a Microchurch Community.
- Disciple: A follower of Jesus who is living green.[231]

---

[228] Matt Ulrich. *Your Discipleship Plan*. The Greenhouse Church, 1. Downloaded: 01/25/2022.
[229] Ibid.
[230] For a more in-depth look see: *Your Discipleship Plan*. bit.ly/dship-path. Downloaded: 01/25/2022.
[231] See: https://greenhousechurch.org/connect/microchurches/leadership-pipeline/. Downloaded: 01/25/2022.

We measure what a disciple is by these minimums:
- *Worship*: Seeking God daily, Sabbath, daily interaction with Scripture
- *Community*: In a MC or discipleship group/Serving in church or microchurch.
- *Mission*: intentionally sharing your faith/reaching out to the lost, giving

- Disciple-Maker: A follower of Jesus who is living green and reproducing that in others.[232]

An invaluable part of discipleship training under Pastor Ulrich involving both becoming a disciple and being a disciple-maker, is to complete the Chartis Assessment, "Your Roadmap to Becoming the Disciple and Disciple-Maker."[233]

Once the disciple or disciple-maker completes The Chartis Assessment, Chartis creates a tailor-made plan for the disciple and/or the disciple-maker. The Chartis Assessment introduces the disciple and/or the disciple-maker to the tools needed to equip disciples and grow in confidence in making disciples.

An invaluable part of discipleship training under Pastor Ulrich, involving both becoming a disciple and being a disciple-maker, is to complete

---

[232] **Defining The Next Steps:**
New Connection Next Step → **Build a Relationship/Have Intentional Conversation** Interested Next Step → **Gauge Their Beliefs/Pre-Salvation Discipleship/Share Gospel**
Believer Next Step → **Get into a Discipleship/MC Community**
Disciple Next Step → **Get Trained**
Disciple Maker Next Step → **Make Disciples**

[233] See: https://chartisassessment.com/. Downloaded: 01/25/2022.

the Chartis Assessment: "Your Roadmap to Becoming the Disciple and Disciple-Maker."[234] Once the disciple or disciple-maker completes the Chartis Assessment, Chartis creates a tailor-made plan for the disciple and/or the disciple-maker.

The Chartis Assessment introduces the disciple and/or the disciple-maker to the tools needed to equip disciples and grow in confidence in making disciples. The Chartis Assessment will instruct the disciple in the following:

- What obedience looks like.
- How to become disciplined in seeking God.
- How to be a part of a real Biblical Community,
- How to live a missional life.
- How to help yourself become healthier and whole.
- How to actually make disciples.

The Chartis Assessment will help disciples map their own personal journey; it will give the disciple practical steps to help them discover significant progress in following Jesus.

Additionally, The Greenhouse Discipleship Assessment[235] "is the best way to assess and get an immediate gauge on where your disciple is at in the areas of worship, mission, community, and disciple-making. It comes

---

[234] Ibid.
[235] Matt Ulrich. Microchurch Pastor. Greenhouse Church. See both: bit.ly/ghdship and https://greenhousediscipleshipassessment.com/. The Chartis and the Greenhouse Discipleship Assessment are functionally the same thing. Chartis was created so people not in the Greenhouse family could utilize an assessment based tool, while the Greenhouse Discipleship Assessment functionally asks the same questions, but with Greenhouse verbiage. While they do vary in some ways, I don't think it is worth repeating/having both off them included.

with an overview of their spiritual journey, over 40 discipleship areas and practical next steps to help them progress in their walk with Jesus, as well as 40 teachings that go along with it. It's truly a one stop shop for both short-term or long-term discipleship relationships as well as a great tool for new disciple-makers or seasoned-ones."[236]

Additional disciplemaking curriculum developed by Pastor Ulrich includes:

- The Green Book[237]: "This book covers all our fluencies here at Greenhouse, so the topics of worship, mission, and community are systematically broken down into fifteen smaller chapters. If you enjoy having a book to read together, this is a great curriculum. There are Scriptures you can both memorize as well as questions throughout each chapter for conversational starting points. This covers the essentials very well to encourage your disciples to be green."[238]
- •Foundations[239]: "This curriculum is a great starting point for anyone who just accepted Jesus. If you like an interactive, fill-in-the-blank style, then this curriculum is for you. It can be done totally together, or parts given as homework to then discuss afterwards. This will help establish some of the theological foundations that every believer needs."[240]

---

[236] Ibid.
[237] Matt Ulrich. The Green Book. bit.ly/greendisciple.
[238] Ibid.
[239] Matt Ulrich. Foundations. bit.ly/greendisciple
[240] Ibid.

- •Discipleship Question Bank[241]: "This is less of a curriculum and more of a way to distill the essence of being a green disciple into a series of questions. There are what we would call ten "essential questions" and then a subsequent bank of questions that are great to ask in a disciple-making setting. These can be used as the primary curriculum of your discipleship group or simply as a good addition to what you are already doing discipleship-wise in general."[242]

"Third Places" (Ch. 16) are among the imaginative ways missional congregations create environments for God to move in the lives of those in spiritual exile and diverse socio-cultural contexts.

---

[241] Matt Ulrich. Discipleship Question Bank. bit.ly/DshipQs Downloaded: 01/25/2022.
[242] Ibid.

CHAPTER 16

"THIRD PLACES"

Alan Hirsch defines "Third Places" by observing that "our first place is the home, our second place is work/school, and our third place is where we spend our time when we have time off."[243] Third places include everywhere "people gather for social reasons. Third places are pubs, cafés, hobby clubs, sports centers, etc. For these communities, 'Church' takes place wherever they are."[244]

EBENEZERS COFFEE HOUSE, WASHINGTON D.C.

"We Serve Coffee with a Cause"

Reflecting on the origins of National Community Church, Mark Batterson, Senior Pastor, recalls the launching of the church on January 7, 1996, a day in which a record-breaking blizzard blanketed Washington D.C. Three people were in attendance, Mark, his wife Lora and their son, Parker. NCC

---

[243] Alan Hirsch. *The Forgotten Ways*. 145.
[244] Ibid.

now (2021) has seven campuses throughout the greater DC metropolitan area.

According to Pastor Batterson, doing church in the middle of the marketplace is a part of NCC's DNA. This observation inspired Batterson's dream of discovering new ways for NCC and their host community, Washington D.C., to daily intersect.

Mark Batterson, the author of the "New York Times" bestselling *Draw the Circle, the 40 Day Prayer Challenge*,[245] describes one "of the crazier dreams we began circling in prayer was to purchase an abandoned building that was once a crack house and build a coffeehouse."[246] 201 F. Street NE is a three-minute walk from Union Station, five and a half blocks from the United States Capitol building and within walking distance from a neighborhood populated by the poor and homeless—Established in 2006, Ebenezars has created a rich blend of environments designed to intersect with and serve the diversified population of D.C.

Pastor Batterson stresses that the "driving motivation behind building a coffeehouse was the fact that Jesus hung out at wells."[247] Wells were gathering places in ancient Near Eastern culture. And third places, like Ebenezers, "is a postmodern well that has served more than a million customers—neighbors, businesspeople, and members of congress alike."[248]

What does Ebenezers[249] mean by, "We serve Coffee with a Cause"? Bill Payne, the manager of Ebenezers, explains that the meaning is layered, but first, it means that all profits support mission efforts in Washington DC and around the world. NCC is driven by a particular core value: "*God will*

---

[245] *Draw the Circle, The 40 Day Prayer Challenge*. Grand Rapids, MI.: Zondervan, 2012.
[246] Pastor Mark Remembers History – NCC https://national.cc/about/our-history
[247] Ibid.
[248] Ibid.
[249] The apostrophe (') is not included in the name of the coffee house.

bless our church in proportion to how we give to missions and care for the poor in our city."[250]

Bill stressed that we are "unapologetic about who we are"—Ebenezers, consistent with the character and compassion of National Community Church, "wants to be more known for what we're for than what we're against. We celebrate each person as invaluable and irreplaceable in the eyes of God because no one can worship God like you or for you. Like Jesus, we love people when they least expect it and least deserve it."[251]

Ebenezers is all about "radical hospitality" through which they create space to make the kingdom of God tangible for the variety of people they celebrate—*Everyone is* included, from some of the most powerful people in the world to outcasts, people unseen by *people who daily pass them by.*

For example, on Wednesday evenings, after normal business hours, Ebenezers hosts the "The Living Room," a homeless outreach. Dinner is provided, a Bible study is open to anyone who wants to participate, and these special guests are made comfortable, they are unconditionally accepted—*"Seeing the unseen" is a way of describing how the homeless are treated with dignity and respect.*

Flowing from "Seeing the unseen," the "Second Mile" service, another Ebenezers' outreach, gathers "the least of these" and seeks to honor and elevate them—How can we go the extra-mile for someone who needs Christ's mercy and compassion?

I asked Bill, "Assuming politics can be toxic and consequently bad for 'business' (much less effective ministry) how does Ebenezers create (or sustain) an apolitical (or close to it) atmosphere?" Bill's answer spoke directly

---

[250] Core Convictions. https://national.cc/about/core-convictions. Downloaded: 07/15/2021.
[251] NCC Our Manifesto. https://national.cc/about/ncc-manifesto. Downloaded: 07/28/2021.

to the power of Christ within us and how service (ministry) is more influential than politics—Bill emphasized that Ebenezers' employees stay faithful to the core values of NCC and consequently, their radical hospitality creates a peaceful environment for civil, friendly conversation, and besides, "Regardless of what you see on cable news stations, these people play softball together!"

A customer service survey of popular coffee houses in Washington D.C. highlighted the great tasting coffee served by nationally known (and some internationally known) coffeehouses in D.C. And although its coffee is among the best, Ebenezers ranked number one in the city for customer service. Ebenezers is intentional about everything it does, especially modeling Christian compassion and service for the "unseen" and the "SEEN" at the intersection of National Community Church and Washington D.C.

THE COFFEE OASIS, BREMERTON, WA[252]

> *"Restoring communities through compassionate youth programs and coffee businesses."*[253]

The Coffee Oasis' story in an unlikely one. The Coffee Oasis originated at the intersection of "smokers' corner" and the hearts of two thoroughly unprepared but extremely compassionate people, Dave, and Cindy Frederick, in 1997. Dave Frederick was raised in a Christian home, but

---

[252] The Burwell Café & Roastery is the original Coffee Oasis ("Hope of Christ") café located in Bremerton, WA. The Bay Street Café is in Port Orchard, WA., the Kingston Café is in Kingston, WA. And the Iverson Café is in Poulsbo, WA. https://thecoffeeoasis.com/cafes/#locations. Downloaded: 11/05/2021.

[253] The Coffee Oasis. https://thecoffeeoasis.com/.

"legalism"[254] framed much of his view of God. The "God" of his childhood loved all people, but didn't seem to especially like gays, lesbians, prostitutes, paroles, drinking, grunge, and tattoos—*In a word, they separated their daily lives from "the world."*

In 1996, the Fredericks started a nonprofit called "Hope in Christ Ministries." The mission of that infant organization was to *bring the hope of Christ to the pain on the streets*. In 1997, Hope in Christ Ministries purchased a failed business called, "The Coffee Oasis." The 1000 square foot location boasted just a couple of regulars, Chris, and Maggie.

Chris and Maggie were both gay and took it upon themselves to help Dave learn the rhythms of community. There were many conversations over coffee where Chris and Maggie educated Dave on the finer points of "this is how you reach us."

Dave should not be thought of as the cover model for missional living. His normal attire of slacks, and a polo shirt was far from relevant. His simple appearance and gentle demeanor would have looked totally alien to the people he deeply wanted to reach.

Trained for overseas mission, Dave knew that to meet people you must go where they are, not expect them to come to you. After months of prayer walking in Bremerton, Dave was pointed to "Smokers' Corner" located across the street from Bremerton High School. Dressed like a "clean-cut"

---

[254] Contrary to liberalism wherein God's Word is subtracted from and replaced by contemporary prevailing cultural norms, "Legalism" essentially involves adding to God's Word in ways that replace God's Word with the opinions or convictions of certain Christians towards contemporary prevailing cultural norms. Legalism conditions the Christian heart to see all the problems and act by placing sharp lines [erecting mental walls] of demarcation between the "holy" and the "unholy." Contrary to the extremes on both sides, while in captivity in Babylon, Daniel the prophet impacted lives, to include the emperor, through wisdom and the separation of his heart unto God and the good (Daniel 1:3-20).

dad from the suburbs, Dave Frederick passed out cheaply made flyers that described The Coffee Oasis as a place for youth to hangout. Four kids from "Smokers' Corner" responded to Dave's invitation that first "Teen Night" in July of 1997. Since that night thousands of youths have walked through the doors of The Coffee Oasis' cafés, shelters and "homes of hope."

At the heart of incarnational mission is relationship. Although Dave was a pastor and a well-educated man, he and Cindy learned about "real relationship" when they opened their home to children in the foster care system, which in-turn led to involvement with the entire family. The Fredericks got to know people "way on the other side of the tracks," far out in the "vacant lots" of the margins. People started coming to the Frederick's home to hear about Jesus, e.g., notorious bikers, prostitutes, drug users and dealers—everyone was welcome. For the first twelve years of Dave's and Cindy's missionally-driven venture, the shelter, soup kitchen, coffee shop and case management for youth was all-volunteer and centered in the Frederick's home.

Daniel Frederick, Dave and Cindy's son and the director of The Coffee Oasis, commented on the different ways youth and young adults (13–25-year-olds) discover Jesus when they come to The Coffee Oasis. When you come, the way incarnation looks to them is shaped by *how* they hear the Jesus story, for example, hearing the story of the woman "caught in the act of adultery" (John 8:3). For many, their focus is on the heartless, judgmental Pharisees, for others, they see a woman without a defense before her accusers, but for many of the broken, emotionally (and physically) scarred youth, they see Jesus *protecting* the woman, even though she had sinned.

Too many people, especially youth, only hear about how bad they are, but they never hear about their value as a person—*Above all else, incarnation means you're wanted.* Just as Dave and Cindy learned from their "mentors" when they opened The Coffee Oasis: *We get to make the invitation, the youth come with all their beauty and pain, and together we meet Jesus.*

As part of his address to The Coffee Oasis supporters at an annual fundraiser, Daniel shared what motivates him, and The Coffee Oasis employees and daily volunteers by sharing quotes from the hearts of troubled kids who left messages on The Coffee Oasis Text Line for Youth:

"The Coffee Oasis has brought a glimpse of hope to my family through such uncertain times."

"I like this program because without it I would have no idea what I was gonna do with my life. It helped me set personal goals and taught me ways to reach these goals"

"Help, I want to kill myself. I'm ugly. I want to get high, cut and die."

"Hi, I'm 13 and I live in Poulsbo. Me and my mom are struggling, and I'm just really stressed."

"I just feel really hopeless about the situation with my mom. She's always overwhelmed with so many things and I can't help but feel like I'm a burden to her."

"I'm 17 years old. I've been having a hard time coping with things and that's leading me to cutting myself. I'm having a bad day and don't know who else to go to. A friend suggested this."

"I am organizing an event to bring awareness of youth suicides. One of my students recently died by suicide. A lot of youth don't know where to go or do not know how to get help."

"I am 23 and have been left in Poulsbo with no money or ID. I need a place to stay until I can find my way back to Oregon. Can you help!?"

"My son needs help. He attempted suicide 2 weeks ago."

"My friend is posting that she wants to die. She tried to jump off the Manette bridge and tried to overdose three times this week and tried to hang herself."

"I can't get a hold of any of my friends, and I just feel like none of them really care. Like I'm a burden and that they just put up with me."

"I feel like my world is crumbling and I give so much to others and never get anything in return except getting screwed over."

"I have my name. I'm 18. I punched my 15-year-old brother. I apologized a lot, and he seems to have forgiven me, but I haven't. Should I turn myself in to the police?"

"I don't have very good people in my life, they hurt me and don't care. Sometimes I think I should just accept the abandonment."

"Hey, I'm having a terrible day. I'm hungry and cold and have nowhere to go and I still want to die. Do things really get better because I have massive doubts? I feel like I've been hearing it's gonna get better all my life and it never has."

"My girlfriend is having a really hard time and I'm worried about her, and I need someone to talk to."

"I'm just overly stressed. There's so much pressure I feel like my head is going to explode. I've spent the last two days in bed ignoring all my problems and they've only gotten worse."

"I tried to commit suicide two months before I left for college."

"A little while ago I had a boyfriend who was older than me and wanted to have sex with me and wanting to keep him still, I agreed to do it even though I knew it would be wrong. Anyways a couple of weeks after me and him broke up because I found out I was pregnant, and he didn't want that on his hands. He forced me to take abortion pills and I lost the baby."

"I've been feeling a bit down lately and I could tell that it's getting worse again. Everything seems dull. I'm willing to give this a try."

"I'm terrified of failing and I'm scared of becoming homeless again. I don't think I would make it out alive or stay drug free this time."

"A few weeks ago, on a band camp trip my friends constantly ignored me. They just kept talking with everyone else in the group. It made me feel like I was either invisible or they didn't care."

"The main thing that's stressing me out right now is my mom. Because of her I don't want to go inside my home. My mom and I have been fighting whenever we talk. I feel really suicidal right now."

"I've never been with anyone that cares about the relationship I have with them. So, there's no freaking point. I just want my ex-boyfriend back, but he doesn't [care] about me. I can't tell him how I feel because he won't call me, and I'll probably never see him again. I'm done."

"Nobody cares about me. I'm a piece of trash that everyone throws away."

"Today is not my day. I dropped a glass, and it broke, and I cut my hand. I hate myself sometimes. I know I complain a lot with this text line, and I feel bad. I don't like bothering you guys with my problems. Or anyone really. I just get tired of holding this all in."

"I don't know if I'm safe. I am a danger to myself."

"I am outside with a man I don't know who keeps trying to have sex with me. He said he would help me go to a church to sleep but took me to a park and keeps touching me. I don't feel safe. He keeps putting his hands on me and says he wants to have sex. I am not from Bremerton and don't know what to do." (Through descriptions we were able to get 911 to her) "The police came and I'm in the hospital. I think I am safe now. Thank you."

September 2021 is a micro-example of how The Coffee Oasis shares in the restoration of young lives: 531 youth were provided bed-nights through housing programs; 854 youth were given access to resources and community at drop-in centers, and 100 individual case management sessions supported youth in achieving their goals.[255]

The Coffee Oasis' many programs "create opportunities for youth to thrive in heart, soul, mind, and strength."[256] The programs are designed and compassionately administered for the sake of helping homeless youth. In many cases, after being kicked out of school, or fleeing from their home for their safety, homeless youth have escaped to the dense forests of the Pacific Northwest.

At The Coffee Oasis, homeless youth find shelter, safety, good food to eat and the means to better health, physically and emotionally, a place in school and the finishing of their education and employment, initially through internships and eventually, long-term, making them responsible, productive, and spiritually grounded, emotionally stable, and members of their community who contribute in meaningful ways that makes other's lives better.[257]

God has given The Coffee Oasis favor with the local justice system, businesses, schools, and political representatives. Daniel pointed to the fact that The Coffee Oasis does things necessary for the health of the community (and with a high-success rate). Evidence of this has been invitations from nearby communities for The Coffee Oasis to expand. (Daniel stressed that other community service providers, churches, and civic organizations have essential services for the health of the community).

---

[255] The Coffee Oasis. https://thecoffeeoasis.com/about/#core. Downloaded: 11/05/2021.

[256] Youth programs at The Coffee Oasis include Hope Home, emergency shelter/supportive housing, Crisis Services, 24-hour text line/substance use counseling, Youth Engagement, outreach/drop-in centers, and Youth Development, case management/mentorship/job training. https://thecoffeeoasis.com/about/#core. Downloaded: 11/05/2021.

[257] Please see The Coffee Oasis's website: https://thecoffeeoasis.com/

THE COFFEE OASIS' ECONOMIC MODEL

The Coffee Oasis' economic model is broken down in three ways: 1/3 of the Coffee Oasis' operations are supported by coffee shops, to include the roasting of The Coffee Oasis' special blends. Another third of The Coffee Oasis' support comes from grants to include, government, foundations, and trusts, the final 1/3 comes from individual, organizational and church donations—*The Coffee Oasis seeks the communities' investment for the heart follows its investments.*

Restoring communities "means impact happening at all levels of community." The greatest asset The Coffee Oasis has is the transformed lives of youth. A significant part of the transformation of youth lives involves internships. Youth internships partner with businesses and the different locations of The Coffee Oasis. Youth participating in internships are awarded monetary stipends for their completion of different phases in their internship.

Youth trained at The Coffee Oasis and other partner businesses are extremely marketable in the community. Following the completion of an internship, Case Managers work diligently with youth to secure employment. During some non-Covid years, 100% of youth were hired within six months following their internships at both Coffee Oasis and local businesses. *The investment of communities in helping youth thrive is faithfully reinvested in communities through transformed youth!*

A FINAL TRIBUTE TO DAVID O. FREDERICK

Dave Frederick, age 66, went to be with Jesus, his Savior, on July 3, 2021, at his home in Bremerton, Washington following a 2 ½ year battle with cancer. Dave's legacy lives-on through the transformed lives of thousands of youths who, apart from Dave and Cindy's willingness to give their lives away to them for God's glory, would have extended their darkened lives into a Christless eternity.

Dave profoundly shaped seemingly countless lives, to include mine as a member of the Board of Directors of The Coffee Oasis for over three years. A final tribute to Dave would be woefully incomplete without acknowledging both his, and Cindy's well-prepared gift to the continuing work of The Coffee Oasis, their son, Daniel Frederick, Director, The Coffee Oasis.

THE BEREAN HOUSE, PE ELL, WA.

Following my honorable discharge from the United States Air Force, I was mentored by a pastor in Seattle, who has now been my pastor for over four decades, Dan Womack. I was, for a season, a youth pastor in Seattle. I failed miserably as a youth pastor, and so, when I and my family were called to a small town in Southwest Washington state to pastor our first church, I initially disagreed with God and His leading of me to the youth of our new community! I felt the need to remind God that I came to Pe Ell, Washington to preach to a handful of old people, not to attempt to reach youth and look terribly foolish [again] in the process!

When I finally acknowledged that I wasn't going to convince an omniscient God of anything, He opened my eyes to a small, vacant house next to our church; I saw why the Lord called me, a very unlikely candidate, to a small town that many people pass through everyday wondering to themselves, "What in the world do people do here?"

Our little church had an annual income of $16,000 and so, when I went to the home of the man who owned the small house, I informed him that our church had $10,000 in savings, and my little congregation told me to offer it all to him, but we needed our monthly payment to be no more than $90.00 a month. The man agreed to our terms and with no money in the bank, and very little operating capital, we launched The Berean House, a youth hangout. (In 1981, I had no idea what a "Third Place" was. I was so "green" and dumb that I didn't realize I was doing something cool like creating a space that sometime in the future would be called a "Third Place"!).

At first only a few youths came to the Berean House to enjoy food, play games and just hangout. Once they began telling their friends, the Berean House began filling up on Friday and Saturday evenings! Youth were really enjoying being together at the Berean House, making youth smile, and even laugh, was new to me, it made me nervous! I decided to set aside a part of the evening and invite any willing youth to watch a Christian film in our small sanctuary next door.

Following the film, I would briefly share the Gospel with youth and most of the time, a couple of them would give their lives to Jesus Christ. On many Sunday afternoons, we would gather as a church at the Chehalis River and baptize youth and celebrate their new creation in Christ! Between the summers of 1981-1982, about 70 youths gave their lives to Jesus Christ, this was more than 10% of the population of our community! (My strategy was to stay out of God's way and just be available for Him to use me!).

On Wednesday evenings I would teach the youth about theology and what it meant to be a Christian. At that time in my Christian life, I had learned more about theological truth from Walter R. Martin's *The Kingdom of the Cults* than any other source I had studied. I would write two passages from cult references and one passage from the Bible; the three sources were about the same subject, and I would ask the youth to identify the counterfeits and tell me about the truth—We began to learn together how to discern truth from counterfeit spiritualities.

We would go on outings—I didn't know we were on "mission"! (We had an old bus that after every trip, I would think that was the last trip it was going to make but it would surprise me, and last for another outing!). In the Spring, I took most of the youth to a convention in the Seattle area. When we returned (following the first time I took the youth to Seattle), the principal at the middle school and high school called me to his office. (It had been a while since I was called to a principal's office, and although none of these "meetings" had been pleasant, I was, nevertheless, on time).

I was informed by the principal that he had to close the middle and high school for the days the youth and I were gone; the absence of a significant portion of the school required the shut-down. (Although the principal was displeased, I thought this was really cool! But I "acted" concerned).

When my family and I prepared to move from Pe Ell so that I could further my education, the administration, the faculty, and the staff at the public school hosted a going away celebration for my wife and me! They saw a profound change in the lives of their students, and they showed their appreciation in a most gracious way (such a celebration by a public school has not happened to my wife and me since, and we have cherished it for over 40 years).

Many of the youth continued to grow in Christ while coupling careers in teaching, police work, and other related public service careers with their faith. (Sadly, many are no longer serving Christ, but I will eventually hunt them all down!). Jesus saved many youth and transformed a small community, and my wife, Vicki, and I will never be the same after being called to Pe Ell, Washington!

CHAPTER 17

COMMON & UNIQUE STRANDS OF MISSIONAL DNA

In 2019, LAPD reported 54,000 car crashes in LA which is almost 150 a day...[258]

On a trip to Africa, I shared many spiritual experiences with a group of pastors. Our trip together was a "paradigm trip" arranged and led by the Northwest Ministry Network, Assemblies of God.

Our paradigm trip took place in East Africa and the Global South. Among the many memorable experiences, was a trip from Addis Ababa,

---

[258] ttps://www.google.com/search?q=how+many+car+accidents+in+los+angeles+per+day&sxsrf=AOaemvJU_5vkQbdTLCuyRMTH6nga9rsQMQ%3A1636839278238&ei=bi-QYeT1DYfO0PEPlYSn0AQ&oq=Number+of+car+accidents+in+los+angeles+per+day&gs_lcp=Cgdnd3Mtd2l6EAEYADIGCAAQFhAeMgUIABCGAzIFCAAQhgMyBQgAEIYDMgUIABCGAzoHCCMQsAMQJzoHCAAQRxCwAzoHCCMQsAIQJzoECCEQCjoFCAAQzQI6BQghEKsCSgUIPBIEMUoECEEYAFD3LlirugFgguUBaAFwAngAgAHoAYgBzBqSAQYyLjI2LjGYAQCgAQHIAQnAAQE&sclient=gws-wiz Downloaded: 11/13/2021.

Ethiopia to Kinshasa, the capital of the Democratic Republic of the Congo in the Global South. Kinshasa is a city of approximately 13 million people. And typical of cities throughout the world, except for North America, Europe and some select cities in other parts of the world, particularly in Asia, traffic flows in a "herd-like" manner, instead of being divided into lanes.

As our van drove through Kinshasa, a couple of the pastors remarked on how surprising it was that they did not see a lot of traffic accidents, after-all, since there are no lanes to divide traffic, everyone seems to drive wherever they please, or so it *appeared* that way.

If you see the world as fragmented or dualistic (sacred/secular divide), your worldview is likely shaped by the "Age of Reason," the French Enlightenment of the 18th century. The "Age of Reason" was concurrent with the founding of the United States of America.[259] Modernism is the Enlightenment's philosophical offspring. Modernism has been a predominant worldview influence for almost two and one-half centuries in North America.

Modernism divides the way we see the world into an incalculable number of components, elements, systems, parts, etc. The net effect of this is, we live in a world sharply (radically) divided into good and evil, right, and wrong, light, and dark, "us" and "them"—Our sense of "separateness" (individualism) requires us to socially "stay in our own lane."

However, the worldviews of most of the earth's population are not shaped by the Enlightenment, they are shaped more by non-dualistic, tribal, and therefore, non-individualistic ways of seeing life and the world (e.g., Kinshasa and The Democratic Republic of the Congo).

---

[259] British Empiricism (Chapter 2) also shaped American thought significantly in her infant political, social, and cultural development.

Acknowledging that my definition of a modernist worldview, and my comments regarding the nature of the worldviews in most of the earth, are brief and therefore, limited, never-the-less, my point is well served: Although the two pastors were surprised to not see a lot of wrecks in the center of Kinshasa, (though undoubtedly there are many wrecks in a city of 13 million people in a typical month), there are many wrecks, as well, in Los Angeles in a typical month. What appears to a Westerner as "chaos," as compared to their "ordered world," is not chaos but rather, it is compatible with the way they see how the world works; life is not divided, it is not dualistic, and therefore, there are "no lanes."

The notion of "no lanes" is more compatible with a biblical worldview, than a Westerner's sense of a philosophically divided world full of "lanes"—To move beyond the first phase (Ch. 2: "Unconscious/Incompetent"), we need to exchange a mindset shaped by the notion that "the line between good and evil," and/or "us" and "them" is an external lane that divides, for a mindset that otherwise realizes "the line between good and evil," and/or "us and them," runs through each one of us—*We need a mindset adaptable to driving in Kinshasa; we need to embrace the reality that missional ministry is post-secular and therefore, initially appears to us (i.e., Westerners) as messy!*

In this sense, it may be said that contrary to modernism's "one size fits all" mindset, missional congregations have a "postmodern quality" about them. But such an assessment errantly [by implication] makes a postmodern hermeneutic "a Bible to the second power."

But, regarding a missional hermeneutic of the Bible, Christopher Wright asserts, "The Bible got there before postmodernity was dreamed of—the Bible which glories in *diversity* and celebrates multiple human *cultures,* the Bible which builds its most elevated theological claims on utterly *particular* and sometimes very *local* events, the Bible which sees everything in *relational,* not abstract, terms, and the Bible which does the bulk of its work through the medium of *stories.*"²⁶⁰ All of these italicized features of Scripture are unhesitatingly received by the postmodern perspective. But the profound point of departure between the postmodern mind and the Bible is that the Bible is, in reality, *"the* story"²⁶¹—The Bible is the "grand narrative that constitutes truth for all...."²⁶² The Bible "is the story of God's mission."²⁶³ The Bible is the "universal story that gives a place in the sun to all the little stories."²⁶⁴

Consequently, in keeping with a missional hermeneutic, whereas missional enterprises share common mDNA, the application of a missional theology by each congregation, organization, and third place, is contextualized and therefore, it [the missional theology] does not necessarily look the same, it is necessarily nuanced.

MISSIONAL DNA STRANDS IN MISSIONAL CONGREGATIONS

> *"It's in the broken pieces that we find the church being reshaped to fit the mission of God in new places, new people and new contexts"*—Brian Sanders.²⁶⁵

---

[260] Christopher Wright. *The Mission of God.* "Searching for a Missional Hermeneutic," 47.
[261] Ibid.
[262] Ibid.
[263] Ibid.
[264] Ibid. Wright references Richard Bauckham's discussion of "the constant biblical oscillation between the particular and the universal, and its implications for a missiological hermeneutic, with special attention to its relevance to postmodernity, in *The Bible and Mission: Christian Mission in a Postmodern World* (Carlisle, U.K.: Paternoster, 2003).
[265] Brian Sanders & Kathryn Eng, "Welcome to the Age of the Microchurch," Interview, https://www.youtube.com/watch?v=Zv7mfGxrx2I. Downloaded: 12/17/2021.

Whereas the following mDNA strands are common to missional congregations, organizations, and third places, they are uniquely applied as a missional theology relative to cultural context, and how each missional enterprise (e.g., congregations, organizations, third places and individual practitioners) sees themselves in relation to the *Missio Dei*:

- **The Lordship of Jesus Christ:** "All authority in heaven and on earth has been given to me"—Jesus Christ is sovereign Lord, He is Alpha and Omega, He is "the great God, the great King" (Ps. 95:3)—A missional congregation's shared identity in Christ, shapes its shared mission; the mission of Jesus Christ.
- **The *Missio Dei*:** The *Missio Dei* originates with the holy Trinity—And God's mission flows into the historical mission of the church. Therefore, "all of life is mission," believers are always on mission, as stressed by Pastor Hoffman, Kaleo Missional Communities, Portland. Whereas Philip, Peter and John were on "proactive mission," that is, a group of missional practitioners sent on mission together to a particular people group, with a clearly defined mission ("proactive mission" is catalytic for disciplemaking, the penultimate purpose of a missional congregation); and "reactive" mission (the individual missional practitioner), involves all of life, all the time, wherever they are.[266]
- **APEST:** The Father sent the Son, and the Father, and the Son sent the Spirit, and the Spirit *sent* the church (Acts 1:8)—A common apostolic strand of DNA is present in these churches, organiza-

---

[266] Although expressed in plural terms, The Mission of National Community Church, Washington D.C., "to do as Jesus did, together, wherever we are" has daily, individual application as well. Core Convictions, National Community Church, https://national.cc/about. Downloaded: 11/13/2021.

tions, and third places.[267] A missional congregation is a church that having "... heard the call to be missional," they "live as people who had been called into the kingdom in order to be sent out."[268]

Greenhouse's theology of microchurches is rooted deeply in Ephesians 4:11—"We're really big on apostle, prophet, evangelist, shepherd and teacher as not just 'seats' in the church but we feel that every believer is equipped with one or more of the APESTs." "We really think that Church is expressed when the APEST is fully functioning... Even with microchurches, is the APEST present?"—"Do you have apostles that are starting things? Do you have prophets that are calling you back to the voice of the Lord? Are evangelists bringing in new people? Are shepherds caring for the flock? Are teachers teaching the Word?" Ephesians 4:11 is a big piece of Greenhouse's, among other missional congregations, theology for microchurches.

> o **Post Secular:** *Missional Ministry is messy*—As Jesus was drawn to the margins to dine with the "unclean," so likewise missional entrepreneurs, delivered from modernity's sacred/secular divide, and defined by sound biblical/missional theology, soar in Christ in desecrated, marginal contexts for the sake of "the others."

The mDNA of the missional congregations, organizations and third places interviewed above cannot be reduced to a series of principles. They do nothing that is formulaic, that is there is no "recipe" for how to be successful like, for example, Father's House in Portland, Jacob's Well in Kansas City, or The Coffee Oasis in Bremerton. They do missional theology in

---

[267] See Alan Hirsch. *The Forgotten Ways,* Section 2: "A Journey to the Heart of Apostolic Genius," 75-ff.
[268] Jim Belcher. *Deep Church, A Third Way Beyond Emerging and Traditional,* 203.

ways that conform to their specific, ever-changing, cultural context; their peculiar identity and consequently, their unique missional theology cannot be duplicated or imitated by another missional congregation in a different zip code (or even the same zip code).

- o **Ecclesial Model:** The ecclesial structure of missional congregations varies, but common traits include: (1) Centralized roles committed to the equipping (spiritual formation, leadership training and media), funding, and encouragement of the decentralized missional operations (the diversified applications of a missional theology), e.g., disciplemaking, missional engagement, both domestic and foreign, and microchurches or a variety of transformational forms of mission.

And (2) Missional Congregations depart from the traditional ecclesial model in varying forms relating to context, mission, and demographics—The missional theology of missional congregations is committed to ecclesial models that serve to empower mission and add value and bring transformation to host communities. Disciplemaking, the penultimate enterprise of missional congregations, is continuingly recurring through decentralized missional operations.

- o **Ancient/Future:** Ancient/Future, in the context of Chapters 8-16, is descriptive of how "the future runs through the past"[269] in missional congregations. The missional "molecule" in the mDNA strands of missional congregations originates within the Holy Trinity (*The Missio Dei*) and is inhered "in Abraham" (Gen. 12:3). And although Israel rejected God's calling to be

---

[269] Robert E. Webber. *Ancient-Future Faith, Rethinking Evangelicalism for a Postmodern World.* Grand Rapids, MI.: Baker Academic, 1999. Preface, 7.

a priestly nation (Ex. 19:5-6), and much of the church has ignored Jesus' summons to be a priestly kingdom (Matt. 28:18-20), the "Priesthood of all Believers" was one of three primary pillars of the Reformation and therefore, Luther contended for its restoration. And finally, following five hundred years, the Priesthood of all Believers resurfaces in "the reformed, always reforming" church (*semper reformanda*), specifically in the mDNA of present-day missional congregations.

- **Creedal:** Like ancient Israel, the church must continually be called back to the voice of the Lord. Missional Congregations prophetically call the body of Christ back to faithfulness to Christian faith, and proper conduct as followers of Jesus Christ. Missional Congregations live in accord with God's Word as it is the foundation of Ancient Creeds or Confessions of the Church, and/or Manifestos (e.g., the Underground), and covenants, e.g., Lausanne Covenant, the Serampore Covenant (William Cary's Ethical Ethos), etc.
- **Fluid:** Missional congregations are fluid (organic), and consequently, they are always adapting; they are always creating new environments for God to work through them in transformative, missionally driven ways. In other words, they don't "drive" in their *own* lane!

MISSIONAL DNA STRANDS

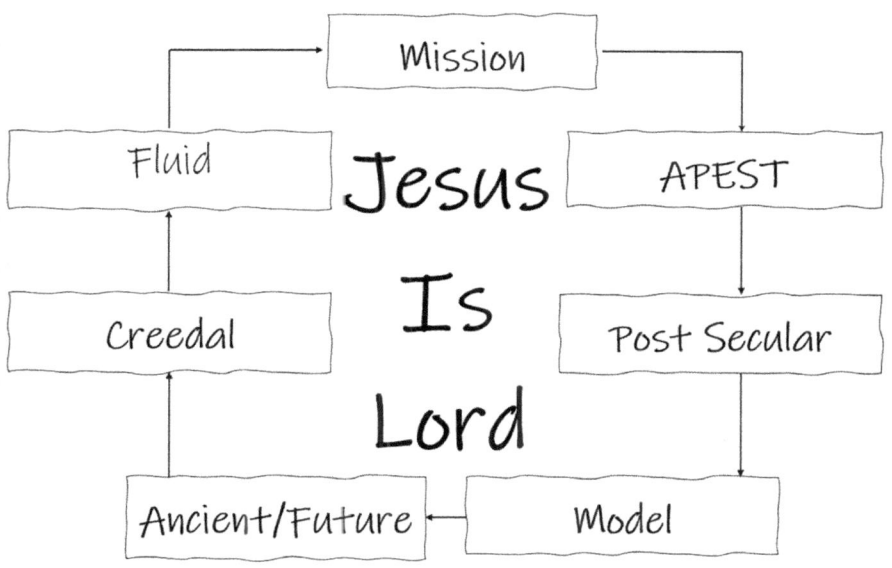

APPENDIX 1

DISCIPLES MAKING DISCIPLES—STAGE 5: "TEACHING THEM TO OBEY..."

Be diligent to present yourself approved to God, a worker who does not need to be ashamed, rightly dividing the word of truth—2 Timothy 2:15 (NKJV)

The websites of the Underground Network, Tampa, Florida (Chapter 8), and Doxa (specifically, "Saturate the Sound"), Bellevue, Washington (Chapter 12), provide access to resources including references (recommended readings), teaching curricula, and videos.[270]

The resources provided by the Underground Network, and Doxa ("Saturate the Sound"), among the other missional congregations and organizations interviewed in chapters 8-16, are critical to their calling to make disciples. And likewise, whereas Section 1, "Disciples Making

---

[270] Please see: The Underground Network, https://www.undergroundnetwork.org/resources and Doxa, https://www.saturatethesound.com/.

Disciples," and Section 2, "Living Missionally Beyond Sunday! Missional Congregations & The Missio Dei," are intended to serve readers in their obedience to make disciples in principle (Section 1) and in practice (Section 2), the work of disciplemaking would be incomplete without Appendix 1, "Teaching Them To Obey." Appendix 1 reintroduces Part 1 and Part 2 of this book and connects them to select resources for a more complete disciplemaking experience.

"TEACHING THEM TO OBEY..."

In Part 1, Chapter 2, "Challenging 'Nest-Bound' Believers," Stage 1 is introduced: "Nest-bound" believers resist joining God on His Mission. Chapter 3, "God's Handiwork," presents Stage 2: *"Born to Fly"*—Coupling Mission and Vocation. Chapter 4, "Mission, Mission, Mission," focuses on Stage 3: *"Modeling Flight"*—liminality and repetitious mission, coupled with modeling, are catalytic for the making of disciples. And Chapter 5, "Incarnational Mission," highlights Stage 4: "Soaring 'In the Zone'"—"The Royal Priesthood" of *all* believers.

Part 2, "Living Missionally Beyond Sunday! Missional Congregations and the *Missio Dei*," is designed to engage the reader in discussion and reflection on how select missional congregations, organizations, and third places practice missional theology.

Disciplemaking is an ongoing process for all disciples, and therefore, the four primary stages of making disciples developed in this book are incomplete without Stage 5, "Teaching Them To Obey." Stage 5 involves ongoing *koinonia* among cohorts of missional-driven disciples with a variety of points of view, mission experiences, and innovations. The following books are selected to develop more fully each stage of disciplemaking discussed in Section 1 of this book. (Selections for each stage of disciplemaking must be consistently updated and added to).

Facilitators meet with cohorts (3 to 10 cohort members) to discuss a select book from each stage. Facilitators should prescribe the number of weeks the cohort will meet to discuss each book. (Generally, cohorts meet 7-8 weeks).[271]

Mission is catalytic for disciplemaking and therefore, cohort participants engage in proactive mission at least once a week. Recommended select readings for each disciplemaking stage is as follows:

STAGE 1: "CHALLENGING NEST-BOUND BELIEVERS"—Living Missionally Beyond Sunday

Steve Addison. *Your Part in God's Story, 40 Days From Genesis to Revelation.* Cody, WY: 100 Movements Publishing, 2021.

Following his triumphant victory over death through his resurrection from the dead, Jesus found his disciples defeated and disillusioned. But after renewing their hope and giving them new vision for a worldwide mission over the course of 40 days, Jesus' disciples were sharing in their Lord's victory!

This book takes the reader through a 40-day journey with Jesus, exploring decisive moments in God's people's lives from Genesis to Revelation—As God's followers discovered their place in his story, so will the reader of this great book!

---

[271] Additional facilitator responsibilities include: (1) The facilitators should understand the difference between a facilitator and a teacher—Facilitators do not lecture or prepare exams for grading but rather they present the subject matter in outline form and prepare questions designed to generate dialogue among cohort members. (Participation among cohort members, instead of passive learning, is critical to discipling missional practitioners). (2) Facilitators develop outcomes and assessments for cohort participants with missional Church leadership (outcomes and assessments should include weekly participation in mission). (3) Meeting times and frequency of meetings vary from church to church depending on cohort members' schedules. (4) The facilitator's team will plan and prepare monthly dinners, for fellowship and relationship building (viz. communitas) among cohort members and facilitators.

Michael W. Goheen. *Reading the Bible Missionally.* Grand Rapids, MI: Wm. B. Eerdmans, 2016.

Biblical and missiological scholars discuss reading the Bible missionally. This book provides examples of missional readings from select chapters in two books, one from the Old Testament and one from the New Testament.

_____. *The Church and its Vocation: Lesslie Newbigin's Missionary Ecclesiology.* Grand Rapids, MI: Baker Academic, 2018.

Lesslie Newbigin's insights regards the church and its place in a pluralistic culture are as relevant today as they were when first written. The author's understanding of Newbigin and his theological convictions enable him to present a clear picture of the church's call to mission in today's world.

_____ **& Craig G. Bartholomew.** *The Drama of Scripture: Finding Our Place in the Biblical Story.* Grand Rapids, MI: Baker Academic, 2014.

This book demonstrates how the grand narrative of the Bible forms the foundation of a Christian worldview. (Please see Baker Academic's Textbook eSources for student study aids, discussion questions, reading schedule and a course syllabus).

Michael Frost & Alan Hirsch. *The Shaping of Things to Come, Innovation and Mission for the 21st – Century Church.* Peabody, MA: Hendrickson Publishers, 2003.

This is a colorful, and innovative engagement with God's missional purposes for His church. The challenges of the 21st century morph into opportunities for the reader as he or she discovers what God is doing throughout Western

Civilization to restore credibility and relevance to Christian faith through missional congregations.

Galen Burkholder & Brother Tefera. *Ordinary Disciples, Extraordinary Influence.* Cody, WY: 100 Movements Publishing, 2022.

This book is filled with biblical insights and miraculous stories of how ordinary disciples live lives of unshakable faith and extraordinary influence in everyday life.

John Harding. *Reflex: The Natural Way to Live the Christian Life.* Cody, WY: 100 Movements Publishing, 2021.

This book is an invitation to live life in a "Jesus-patterned way"—The Christian life is a life of freedom and fruitfulness that transforms the lives of others around us!

Daryl L. Smith & Andrew B. Smith. *Discovering Your Missional Potential: A Village Group Encounter with Ephesians 4 and How Jesus Lives It.* Cody, WY: 100 Movements Publishing, 2019.

God has gifted all believers to participate in God's mission of transformation, renewal and restoration in the world. Our missional calling begins with our discovery of how God has gifted us individually and as community in relation to Ephesians 4, APEST.

Barna Group. *Gen Z: The Culture, Beliefs and Motivation Shaping the Next Generation.* 1st Edition, 2018.

The Barna Group produced this informative book in partnership with 360 Institute. Gen Z is the 13–18-year-old age group. This book discusses the perceptions, experiences, and motivations of Gen Z. The research for this book is based on interviews and analysis.

_____. *Gen Z: Vol. 2, The Culture, Beliefs and Motivation Shaping the Next Generation.* 2021.

The Gen Z generation was born between 1999 and 2015. When Vol. 1 was written, the oldest members of Gen Z were barely 17. Vol 2 continues to track this "driven, informed, hopeful-but-skeptical, spiritually open, highly connected, anxious generation." Vol 2 was also developed in partnership with Impact 360 Institute.

STAGE 2: *"BORN TO FLY"*—COUPLING MISSION & VOCATION

Rowland Smith. *Life Out Loud, Joining Jesus Outside the Walls of the Church.* Cody, WY: 100 Movements Publishing, 2019.

Rowland Smith had experienced long-term, fruitful ministry within the church, but he became convinced that there has to be more! Rowland Smith discovered that there was more by joining Jesus outside of the church, among people who are not seeking Jesus—But Jesus is seeking them through believers like Rowland!

The author engages the reader with sound, practical theology, personal reflection, and experiential knowledge—If you dare to read this book, prepare yourself for "your own life out loud!"

Alan Hirsch & Mark Nelson. *Reframation, Seeing God, People, and Mission Through Reenchanted Frames.* Cody, WY: 100 Movements Publishing, 2019.

Reframation is a clarion call to Jesus' followers to "reframe and reenchant" how we see God's grand story all around us—This book presents the Gospel in ways that resonates with the spiritual hunger and soulful longings of the exiled in our contemporary culture.

John Stott. *Mission: Rethinking Vocation.* Vancouver B.C.: Regent College Publishing, 2019.

John Stott rethought the significance of vocation and its coupling with mission thoroughly, no doubt, long before most. This renown theologian, prolific writer and faithful pastor is a voice the wise listen intently to.

Robert E. Fraser. *Marketplace Christianity: Discovering the Kingdom Purpose of the Marketplace.* Overland Park, KS: New Grid Publishing, 2004.

Experienced entrepreneur, Robert Fraser, provides invaluable insight into how he was used by Christ to sustain a revival, alongside of business success, during his tenure as CEO of a 250-employee software company—Fraser's passion is to engage "business owners with a vision for financing the world harvest."

Alan Scott. *Scattered Servants: Unleashing the Church to Bring Life to the City.* Elgin, ILL: David C. Cook, 2018.

An outstanding work testifying to the power of the Holy Spirit working in and through the life of every believer to transform cities, the marketplace, and neighborhoods.

Darren Shearer. *The Marketplace Christian: A Practical Guide to Using Your Spiritual Gifts in Business.* Houston, TX: High Bridge Books, 2015.

The Marketplace Christian is both practical and personalized by way of presenting strategies that enable believers in the business world to discover how, through God's gifting of them, they are equipped to transform the marketplace. This book provides a "Spiritual Gifts in the Marketplace" assessment for readers. An outstanding book for cohorts!

Michael W. Goheen & Jim Mullins. *The Symphony of Mission: Playing Your Part in God's Work in the World.* Grand Rapids, MI: Baker Academic, 2019.

Every believer lives with missional intentionality by understanding the many sides of mission and realizing a particular calling. Like the different instruments in an orchestra that harmonize together, this book helps readers to imagine how their calling (their instrument) is necessary to the harmony of God's mission.

Alec Hill. *Just Business. Christian Ethics for the Marketplace*, 3rd Edition. Downers Grove, IL: Inter-Varsity Press Academic, 2018.

This book provides case studies of common responses to business ethics and how they fall short of a Christian worldview. Hill demonstrates how God's character, primarily, holiness, justice, and love, is foundational for Christian ethics.

Center for Christianity in Business & Ernest P. Liang, Editor. *Christianity in Business: Applying Biblical Values in the Marketplace (Biblical Worldview and the Marketplace Series).*

Valuable insights are offered on the theme of work-place integration—For a Christian, business is not merely a way of making a living, it is a sacred part of living a fully integrated life as a citizen of the kingdom of God.

Leonard Sweet. *Post-Modern Pilgrims: First Century Passion for the 21st Century.* Nashville, TN: Broadman & Holman Publishers, 2000.

Typical of Leonard Sweet's writing, the theme of this book—a biblical view of the tension between tradition and innovation and how they work together to strengthen and mature the church—is not only very conspicuous, but it is throughout, illustrative, and exhilarating!

STAGE 3: MISSION, MISSION, MISSION—*MODELING FLIGHT*

Alan Hirsch. *The Forgotten Ways*. Grand Rapids, MI: Brazos Press, 2006.

Alan Hirsch's, The Forgotten Ways, is the definitive statement on missional praxis and the power of movements, historically and for the future of the church.

Michael Frost. *Surprise the World: The Five Habits of Highly Missional People.* Colorado Springs, CO: NavPress, 2016.

The missional practitioner is always on mission, and therefore, we are always prepared to evangelize, both in word and the way we live. Surprise the World employs the "BELLS Method" to witness for Christ: **Bless** *others;* **Eat** *together;* **Listen** *to the Spirit;* **Learn** *Christ. This book makes evangelism exciting, fulfilling, and effective!*

Leonard Sweet. *Me & We, God's New Social Gospel.* Nashville, TN: Abington Press, 2014.

Unlike the naïve notions of the "Social Gospel" in the 19th and/or 20th centuries, God's new Social Gospel is driven by the Wesleyan impulse "to proclaim freedom for the prisoners and recovery of sight for the blind… to set the oppressed free by faith in Jesus Christ."

Jon Ritner. *Positively Irritating, Embracing a Post-Christian World to Form a More Faithful and Innovative Church.* Cody, WY: 100 Movements Publishing, 2020.

Cultural seismic plates are shifting rapidly beneath the surface of everyday life in Western Civilization—Driven by Marxist cultural ideology, secularism, scientism, and materialism are succeeding in exiling any spiritual explanation for life. But rather than seeing these challenges as problems, Jon Ritner sees them as opportunities to embrace. Christians need to exchange traditional disciplemaking strategies that rely on programs for one that empowers God's people to join Him on mission and make disciples in and through the rhythms of everyday life.

Paul M. Gould. *Cultural Apologetics, Renewing the Christian Voice, Conscience, and Imagination in a Disenchanted World.* Grand Rapids, MI: Zondervan, 2019.

Our post-Christian culture is disenchanting, it is void of beauty and mystery. And tragically, the church has conformed rather than confronted—"The Christian church has grown anti-intellectual and sensate, out of touch with the relevancy of Jesus and how to relate the gospel to all aspects of contemporary life" (From the back cover of *Cultural Apologetics, Renewing the Christian Voice, Conscience, and Imagination in a Disenchanted World*).

This book confronts our disenchanted world in the spirit of Paul's confrontation of the Stoics and the Epicureans on Mars Hill—Gould presents the Christian faith for what it is, reasonable, and desirable, a renewed vision of enchantment, beauty, and imagination.

Jeff Vanderstelt. *Gospel Fluency: Speaking the Truths of Jesus into the Everyday Stuff of Life.* Wheaton, ILL: Crossway, 2017.

To become fluent in a foreign language, we must immerse ourselves in it until we begin seeing life through it. Vanderstelt explains that our fluency in the Gospel happens in the same way—We need to immerse ourselves in the truths of the Gospel and rehearse our delivery to both ourselves and others until we begin to live, "from the mundane to the magnificent" through the hope of the Gospel.

Dietrich Bonhoeffer. *The Cost of Discipleship.* New York, N.Y.: Touchstone (First Edition, 1995).

Bonhoeffer's seminal work was first published in Germany, 1937—This book's title is not hyperbole, to the contrary, Bonhoeffer lived the disciple's life, and taught others how to as well, until the day of his martyrdom.

Bonhoeffer draws on the disciplined life of the Sermon on the Mount—In the first three centuries of the church, the Sermon on the Mount was regarded as the centerpiece of Jesus' teaching and therefore, it was a primary source for Christian discipleship/formation. Throughout the Sermon on the Mount, Jesus expounds on how the radiance of the church (the church's "better righteousness," Bonhoeffer) gives light to the reality of the present kingdom.

_____. *Life Together, The Classic Exploration of Christian Community.* New York, NY: Harper-Collins Publishers, 1954.

A martyr at the hands of the Third Reich for his part in plotting to assassinate Hitler, Dietrich Bonhoeffer's faith and courage makes his work, to include Life Together cherished testimony. In this book, Bonhoeffer writes about true community (communitas) in an underground seminary during the Nazi control of Germany—Life Together is "bread for all who are hungry" for real Christian fellowship.

Brian Sanders. *The Six Seasons of Calling: Discovering Your Purpose in Each Stage of Life.*

Chicago, ILL: Moody Publishers, 2022.

The six seasons of calling include:

- *Childhood—The season of bonding*
- *Adolescence—The season of leaning*
- *Early Career—The season of serving*
- *Mid-Career—The season of creating*

- *Late Career—The season of giving*
- *Transition—The season of leaving*

The author encourages us to locate ourselves in each season of life, and learn mindfully in each season, and learn from its lessons. And look for what's next and keep in mind, only at the end of your life, will you learn the value of each season and why life should not be rushed.

David Kinnaman & Mark Matlock. *Faith for Exiles:5 Ways for a New Generation to Follow Jesus in Digital Babylon.* Grand Rapids MI: Baker Books, 2019.

Faith for Exiles is about five practices among "church dropouts, prodigals and nomads" that contribute to their sustaining faith. This book's research and testimony to God's faithfulness to young disciples today is encouraging!

STAGE 4: "SOARING 'IN THE ZONE'"—INCARNATIONAL MISSION

Samuel Wells. *Incarnational Mission, Being with the World.* Grand Rapids, MI: Wm. B. Eerdmans, 2018.

Samuel Wells clearly explains the meaning behind mission-minded churches and believers "being with the world."

Robert A. Multhiah. *The Priesthood of all Believers in the 21st Century: Living Faithfully as the Whole People of God in a Postmodern Context.* Eugene, OR: Pickwick Publishers, 2009.

This book argues for renewed embracing of Luther's teaching on the Priesthood of all Believers in the 21st century Postmodern context. The author creates dialogue between ecclesiology, postmodern culture, and congregational practices.

Brian Sanders. *Underground Church, A Living Example of the Church in its Most Potent Form.*

Grand Rapids, MI: Zondervan, 2018.

Underground Church is an "ancient-future" vision of empowerment for a priesthood of believers let loose in a city to bring transformation through the power of the Spirit and the Word—Sanders introduces structural changes, thoughts about leadership, funding ministries, and how to empower the 20% to meet needs, and bring hope to those in exile.

_____. *Microchurches, (A Smaller Way).* 2019.

"Perhaps, after all our hand wringing and insecurity about the size of our churches, we have missed the point. Microchurches can be strong, beautiful, accessible, and potent portraits of just what Jesus had in mind, if not for all time, at least for ours"—From the back cover of *Microchurches (A Smaller Way).*

Alan Hirsch. *5Q: Reactivating the Original Intelligence and Capacity of the Body of Christ.* Cody, WY. 100 Movements Publishing, 2017.

In 5Q: Reactivating the Original Intelligence and Capacity of the Body of Christ, Alan Hirsh engages the APEST in Ephesians 4:1-16. Hirsch's profound theological, cultural insight, and innovation persuasively (and wisely) redefines our understanding of calling, church, leadership, and organization.

_____ and Jesse Cruickshank. *Activating 5Q: A User's Guide.*

This User's Guide is designed to equip missional congregations and individual practitioners to practically "live into a new way of seeing, thinking, and living" out the principles articulated in 5Q in their contexts.

John R. Franke. *Missional Theology, An Introduction.* Grand Rapids, MI: Baker Academic, 2020.

John R. Franke discloses a clear understanding of missional theology as he demonstrates the flow of mission from God and His purposes for missional congregations. Franke examines the implications of missional theology, e.g., plurality and multiplicity.

Leonard Sweet. *Rings of Fire, Walking in Faith Through a Volcanic Future.* Colorado Springs, CO: Nav Press, 2019.

Among mortals, Leonard Sweet possesses the most creative mind I have ever known. Leonard Sweet's prophetic insight guides the reader through current cultural challenges that point to future spiritual-social impact. Throughout his writing, Leonard Sweet lifts the eyes of the reader to Jesus Christ for hope and assurance.

Christopher J.H. Wright. *The Mission of God, Unlocking the Bible's Grand Narrative.* Downers Grove, ILL: Inter-Varsity Press, 2006.

This book is quoted often throughout Living Missionally Beyond Sunday!— The Mission of God is the primary reference work for missional theology and living. This is a voluminous work and therefore, a facilitator is encouraged to go to it often as he or she guides a cohort through missional understanding and growth. If used for a cohort, the facilitator should select chapters for cohort reading and discussion (It is highly recommended that all serious-minded missional practitioners become familiar with this great work).

Charlie Self. *Flourishing Churches and Communities: A Pentecostal Primer on Faith, Work, and Economics for Spirit-Empowered Discipleship.* Grand Rapids, MI.: Christian Library Press, 2012.

Dr. Self provides a vivid picture of what it looks like for followers of Jesus to take the Great Commandment and the Great Commission seriously in the context of their own local communities. Charlie focuses on the need to integrate faith, work, and economics as critical to the task of making disciples. This primer aims at wholehearted discipleship that extends beyond our Sundays at church and into our workplaces the rest of the week.

Robert E. Webber. *Ancient-Future Faith, Rethinking Evangelicalism for a Postmodern World.* Grand Rapids, MI: Baker Academic, 1999.

The present must find passage through the ancient if it is going to speak to the postmodern world. Webber relies on the transforming power of the Gospel as the evangelical church's primary arsenal in facing the cultural challenges of our day.

BIBLIOGRAPHY

Acton Institute: "Our Mission & Core Principles." https://www.acton.org/about/mission. Downloaded: 10/27/2021.

Augustine. *The City of God.* Edited: Whitney J. Oates. *Basic Writings of Saint Augustine.* Volume Two. Grand Rapids, MI: Baker Book House, Reprinted: 1992.

Barna Group & Abilene Christian University. *Christians at Work, Examining the Intersection of Calling & Career.* Barna Group, 2018.

Barna Group. *Better Together, How Christians Can Be a Welcome Influence in Their Neighborhoods.* Barna Group, 2020.

Batterson, Mark. *Draw the Circle, The 40 Day Prayer Challenge.* Grand Rapids, MI.: Zondervan, 2012.

Bauer, Walter, Arndt, William, Gingrich, Wilbur F., and Danker, Frederick W. *A Greek-English Lexicon of the New Testament and Other Early Christian Literature.* Chicago, IL.: The University of Chicago Press, 1958.

Bauckham, Richard. *The Bible and Mission: Christian Mission in a Postmodern World.* Carlisle, U.K.: Paternoster, 2003.

Belcher, Jim. *Deep Church, A Third Way Beyond Emerging and Traditional,* 203.

Berry, Wendell. "There Are No Sacred and Unsacred Places https://kimmysophiabrown.com/mo-bliss/a-contemplation-of-nature-and-spirituality/wendell-berry-there-are-no-sacred-and-unsacred-places/. Downloaded 10/22/2021.

Bonhoeffer, Dietrich. *The Cost of Discipleship*. New York, N.Y.: Simon & Schuster, 1959.

_____. *Life Together: The Classic Exploration of Christian Community*. Harper & Row Publishers, Inc., 1954.

Brown, F.S.R., Driver, and C.A. Briggs. *A Hebrew and English Lexicon*. Oxford: Clarendon, 1907.

Broge, Jason. "Affective Learning: How Congregants Move from Passion to Action." *Better Together, How Christians Can be a Welcome Influence in Their Neighborhoods*. Barna Group, 2020.

Carroll R., M. Daniel. *Blessing the Nations: Toward a Biblical Theology of Mission from Genesis. Bulletin for Biblical Research 10.1 (2000)*. file:///C:/Users/theWr/AppData/Local/Packages/Microsoft.MicrosoftEdge_8wekyb3d8bbwe/TempState/Downloads/BBR_2000_a_02_Carroll_BlessingTheNations%20(1).pdf. Downloaded: 04/10/2019.

Crossan, John Dominic. *In Parables. The Challenge of the Historical Jesus*. Sonoma, CA.: Polebridge Press, 1992.

Discipleship Dynamics LLC. *Discover, Define, Disciple*. Springfield, MO. 4319 S. National #207, 65810. https://discipleshipdynamics.com/about-the-assessment/#economics-work. Downloaded: 10/19/2021.

Discipleship Dynamics. Coaching and Consulting. https://discipleshipdynamics.com/coaching-and-consulting/. Downloaded: 10/27/2021.

Faith & Works Center, Vision, https://faithandwork.com/about/. Downloaded: 10/25/2021. Faith & Works Centers affiliated with FWC, New York, Redeemer Presbyterian Church.

Global Faith & Work Initiative, A Ministry of "Redeemer City to City." https://www.globalfaithandwork.com/resources Downloaded: 08/24/2020.

Greear, J.D. pastor, The Summit Church, Raleigh-Durham, NC. https://jdgreear.com/blog/martin-luther-on-gods-masks/. Downloaded: 12/12/2019.

Fee, Gordan. *The New International Commentary on the New Testament, The First Epistle to the Corinthians.* Grand Rapids, MI.: William B. Eerdmans Publishing Co., 1987.

Forge America, http://www.forgeamerica.com/. Downloaded: 07/15/2019.

Forge America Training Manual, Section 2, "The Local Forge Hub," 16, http://www.forgeamerica.com/, Downloaded: 07/12/2019.

Kittel, Gerhard, Editor. *Theological Dictionary of the New Testament.* Volume II. Translated by: Geoffrey W. Bromiley. Grand Rapids, MI.: Eerdmans, 1964.

_____. *Theological Dictionary of the New Testament.* Volume III. Translated by: Geoffrey W. Bromiley. Grand Rapids, MI.: Eerdmans, 1965.

Friedrich, Gerhard and Kittel, Gerhard, Editors. *Theological Dictionary of the New Testament.* Volume V. Translated by: Geoffrey W. Bromiley. Grand Rapids, MI.: Eerdmans, 1967.

_____. *Theological Dictionary of the New Testament.* Volume VI. Translated by: Geoffrey W. Bromiley. Grand Rapids, MI.: Eerdmans, 1968.

_____. *Theological Dictionary of the New Testament.* Volume VII. Translated by: Geoffrey W. Bromiley. Grand Rapids, MI.: Eerdmans, 1971.

_____. *Theological Dictionary of the New Testament.* Volume IX. Translated by: Geoffrey W. Bromiley. Grand Rapids, MI.: Eerdmans, 1974.

Frost, Michael & Alan Hirsch. *The Shaping of Things To Come.* Peabody, MA.: Hendrickson Publishers, 2003. 35.

Harris, R. Laird, Archer, Gleason L. Jr., and Waltke, Bruce K. *Theological Wordbook of the Old Testament,* Vol. I (Chicago, IL.: Moody Press, 1980).

_____. *Theological Wordbook of the Old Testament,* Vol. II (Chicago, IL.: Moody Press, 1980).

Hathcock, Jeff. Barstool Pastor, "Our Story," https://www.facebook.com/pg/barstool.pastor/about/?ref=page_internal. Downloaded, 01/14/2019.

Hill, Clifford. *The Wilberforce Connection.* Oxford, UK, Monarch, 2004.

Hirsch, Alan. *The Forgotten Ways.* Grand Rapids, MI.: Brazos Press, 2006.

_____. & Deb, Frost, Michael. Forge International Website http://www.forgeinternational.com/about#our-story downloaded, 07/15/2019.

_____. "What is Missional Discipleship?" https://www.youtube.com/watch?v=WhEwxSQ5tqA. Downloaded: 02/28/2019.

Jacobs. C.M. (*Works of Luther,* Philadelphia: A. J. Holman Company, 1915*),* found online at: http://www.iclnet.org/pub/resources/text/wittenberg/luther/web/nblty-03.html

Jacob's Well. https://www.jacobswellchurch.org/. Downloaded: 06/07/2021.

_____. https://www.jacobswellchurch.org/ WATCH/LISTEN. Downloaded: 09/22/2021.

Kaiser, Jr., Walter C. "The Great Commission in the Old Testament," page 4 of 7 pages. file:///C:/Users/theWr/AppData/Local/Packages/Microsoft.MicrosoftEdge_8wekyb3d8bbwe/TempState/Downloads/01_Kaiser%20(1).pdf Downloaded: 04/10/019

Keller, Tim. "Discerning Your Calling," https://www.whatsbestnext.com/2011/08/tim-keller-on-discerning-your-calling/, August 23, 2011. Downloaded: 02/20/2019.

Lewis, C.S. *The Quotable Lewis.* Editors: Wayne Martindale & Jerry Root. Wheaton, IL.: Tyndale House Publishers, Inc. 1990.

Lindsey, Art. Institute for Faith, Work & Economics. "The Priesthood of all Believers." https://tifwe.org/resource/the-priesthood-of-all-believers/ Downloaded, 07/06/2019.

Louw, Johannes P., and Eugene A. Nida. *Greek-English Lexicon of the New Testament, Based on Semantic Domains.* Two Volumes,

Luther on God's 'Masks,' Martin Luther's exposition of Psalm 147. Posted August 29, 2012, The Rev 2011 in Church History, Providence, Reformed Piety & Christian Nurture. https://christcovenantopc.wordpress.com/2012/08/29/luther-on-gods-masks/. Downloaded: 12/12/2019

Luther, Martin. "Open Letter to the Christian Nobility of the German Nation Concerning the Reform of the Christian Estate (1520),"

_____. *The Sermon on the Mount.* 1521. Translated by Jaroslav Pelikan. Vol. 21 of *Luther's Works.* Concordia, 1956.

Made to Flourish: https://www.madetoflourish.org/ Downloaded: 04/05/2019.

McRoberts, Kerry D. *A Letter from Christ, Apologetics in Cultural Transition.* Lanham, MD.: University Press of America, INC. 2012

_____. *Insanity! How Can Sanity and Civility be Restored to a Culture in the Process of Being Turned Over to Itself?* Eugene, OR.: Resource Publications/Wipf and Stock Publishers, 2018.

_____. *Following Jesus to Burning Man, Recovering the Church's Vocation.* (Hamilton Books, 2011).

McRoberts, Vicki R. The five eagle images, e.g., the "Nest-Bound Eagle," the "Vocational Eagle," the "Liminal Eagle," the "Soaring eagle," and the "Professor [Facilitator] Eagle," are the creations of Vicki McRoberts, "Intrinsic Doodles Inc." (Re: Chapter 6, "Living Missionally Beyond Sunday! Principles In The mDNA of Missional Congregations").

Missional University: https://missional.university/

National Community Church. Core Convictions. https://national.cc/about/core-convictions. Downloaded: 07/15/2021.

_____: Our Manifesto. https://national.cc/about/ncc-manifesto. Downloaded: 07/28/2021.

National Human Trafficking Hotline, Ranking of the Most Populus US Cities, 12/7/2007 – 12/31/2016.https://humantraffickinghotline.org/sites/default/files/100%20Most%20Populous%20Cities%20Report.pdf. Downloaded: 02/12/2021.

Neurons and Electrons Images: https://www.shutterstock.com/search/neutrons+and+electrons. Downloaded:

Newbigin, Lesslie. *Missionary Theologian,* A Reader. Extract 1, "Evangelism and the City," (1987). Compiled by: Paul Westin. Grand Rapids, MI. Wm. B. Eerdmans, 2006. 144.

Packer, J.I. *Knowing God.* Downers Grove, IL.: Inter-Varsity Press, 1973

Robertson, Archibald Thomas. *Word Pictures in the New Testament.* Volume I, Matthew & Mark. Grand Rapids, MI.: Baker Book House, 1930 (Sunday School Board of the Southern Baptist Convention).

_____. *Word Pictures in the New Testament.* Volume II, Luke. Grand Rapids, MI.: Baker Book House, 1930 (Sunday School Board of the Southern Baptist Convention).

_____. *Word Pictures in the New Testament.* Vol. III, The Acts of the Apostles. Grand Rapids, MI.: Baker Book House, 1930 (Sunday School Board of the Southern Baptist Convention).

_____. *Word Pictures in the New Testament.* Volume IV, Epistles of Paul. Grand Rapids, MI.: Baker Book House, 1931 (Sunday School Board of the Southern Baptist Convention).

_____. *Word Pictures in the New Testament.* Volume V, The Fourth Gospel & The Epistle to the Hebrews. Grand Rapids, MI.: Baker Book House, 1932 (Sunday School Board of the Southern Baptist Convention).

_____. *Word Pictures in the New Testament.* Volume VI, General Epistles & Revelation. Grand Rapids, MI.: Baker Book House, 1933 (Sunday School Board of the Southern Baptist Convention).

Robinson, Martin. & Dwight Smith. *Invading Secular Space.* Oxford, U.K.: Monarch, 2003.

Ross, Don. "Theology of Change – A Message from Network Leader, Don Ross." https://vimeo.com/412477594. Downloaded: 05/04/2020.

Roxburgh, Alan J. & Romannuk, Fred. *The Missional Leader.* San Francisco, CA.: Jossey-Bass, 2006.

Sanders, Brian & Kathryn Eng. "Welcome to the Age of the Microchurch," Interview, https://www.youtube.com/watch?v=Zv7mfGxrx2I. Downloaded: 12/17/2021.

Sanders, Brian. *Microchurches, (A Smaller Way).* Tampa Bay, FL.: Underground Media, 2019.

_____. *Underground Church, a living example of the church in its most potent form.* Grand Rapids, MI.: Zondervan, 2018.

SATURATE THE SOUND. "The World Waits for Followers of Jesus to be Authentic and Inspiring." https://www.saturatethesound.com/. Downloaded: 06/11/2021.

Sayers, Dorothy. "The Secular Vocation is Sacred, Serve God in Your Profession, Not Outside It." April 1942. https://renovare.org/articles/the-secular-vocation-is-sacred. Downloaded: 10/05/2021.

Schaeffer, Francis A. Book Two: *Escape from Reason*. The Complete Works of Francis A. Schaeffer, A Christian Worldview. Volume 1, A Christian View of Philosophy and Culture. Second Edition. Westchester, Illinois, Crossway Books, 1982.

Schmidgall, David. National Community Church, Lincoln Theatre Campus Pastor. "Partnering in the Mission of Jesus." https://national.cc/media/disciple/partnering-in-the-mission-of-jesus. Downloaded: 09/24/2021.

Self, Charlie. Discipleship Dynamics. Coaching and Consulting. https://discipleshipdynamics.com/coaching-and-consulting/. Downloaded: 10/27/2021.

SOMA. Saturate Equipping. https://wearesoma.com/saturate-equipping/. Downloaded: 06/04/2021.

Stassen, Glenn & Gushee, David. *Following Jesus In Contemporary Context, Kingdom Ethics*. Downers Grove, IL.: InterVarsity Press, 2003.

Stott, John. *The Contemporary Christian: Applying God's Word To Today's World*. Downers Grove, Ill.: InterVarsity Press, 1992.

The Coffee Oasis. https://thecoffeeoasis.com/.

_____. https://thecoffeeoasis.com/about/#core. Downloaded: 11/05/2021.

The Manifesto and Values of the Underground, see: Tampa Underground Network. https://www.tampaunderground.com/our-story-index-#manifesto-intro. Who We Are/Values. Downloaded: 12/17/2021.

_____: https://www.tampaunderground.com/

_____: https://vimeo.com/256315051

_____: https://www.undergroundnetwork.org/who-we-are-index/#new-model. Downloaded: 12/08/21.

_____: https://www.undergroundnetwork.org/who-we-are-index/#new-model. Downloaded: 12/08/21.

_____. https://www.tampaunderground.com/resources. Downloaded: 12/18/2021.

Vanderstelt, Jeff. "Baptismal Identity," Baptismal Identity Jeff Vanderstelt HD - YouTube. Downloaded: 02/06/2021.

_____. *Building A Missional Community*, Part 1. https://www.youtube.com/watch?v=x8Inw0YchwM, Downloaded: 02/05/2019.

_____. "How to Equip a Missional Community Series Sample/ How to Form a Missional Community/Soma. https://www.youtube.com/watch?v=ufPjFq66_OU&t=731s. Downloaded: 02/06/2021.

Veith, Dr. Gene Edward. Director of the Cranach Institute. "Masks of God." Downloaded 12/12/2019. http://mothersarehome.blogspot.com/2011/12/masks-of-god.html.

Watson, Brad. *Multiply Together, A Guide to Sending and Coaching Missional Communities*. GCD Books, 2016.

_____. And Jonathan K. Dodson. *Called Together, A Guide to Forming Missional Communities*. Austin, TX.: GCD Books, 2014.

_____. *Sent Together, How the Gospel Sends Leaders to Start Missional Communities*. Second Edition. GCD Books, 2015.

Webber, Robert E. *Ancient-Future Faith, Rethinking Evangelicalism for a Postmodern World*. Grand Rapids, MI.: Baker Academic, 1999.

Wells, Samuel. *Incarnational Mission, Being With the World*. Grand Rapids, MI.: William B. Eerdmans Publishing Company, 2018.

Willard, Dallas. *Divine Conspiracy*. San Francisco, CA.: Harper, 1997.

Wright, Christopher J.H. *The Mission of God, Unlocking the Bible's Grand Narrative.* Downers Grove, IL.: Inter-Varsity Press, 2006.

_____. "Truth with a Mission: Reading All Scripture Missiologically." file:///C:/Users/theWr/AppData/Local/Packages/Microsoft.MicrosoftEdge_8wekyb3d8bbwe/TempState/Downloads/2_sbjt-v15-n2_wright%20(1).pdf. Downloaded 04/13/2019

Wright, N.T. *After You Believe, Why Christian Character Matters.* New York, N.Y.: Harper-One, 2010.

_____. *Jesus and the Victory of God.* Minneapolis, MN.: Fortress Press, 1996.

_____. *Paul, A Biography.* New York, NY.: HarperOne, 2011.

_____. Same-Sex Marriage. https://www.youtube.com/watch?v=x-KxvOMOmHeI. Downloaded: 04/19/2019.

_____. *The Challenge of Jesus: Rediscovering Who Jesus Was and Is.* Downers Grove, IL.: InterVarsity, 1999.

_____. *The New Testament and the People of God.* Minneapolis, MN.: Fortress, 1992.

www.ingramcontent.com/pod-product-compliance
Lightning Source LLC
LaVergne TN
LVHW051551070426
835507LV00021B/2522